The Little Boy Asked Why?

The Search for Answers.

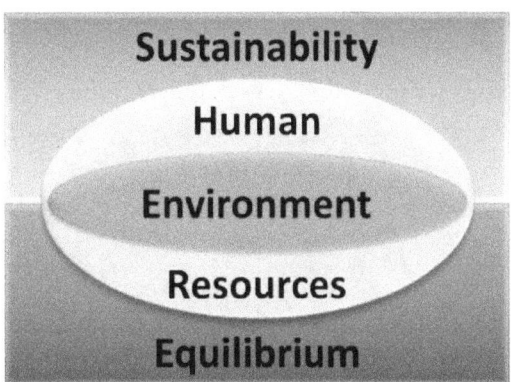

Wayne L Staley

Dedications

To:

To the Citizens of the United States of
America, all deserve an opportunity
driven society.

To the courageous young people who
will push back against the national drift
into an Orwellian dystopia, or eventually
live in one.

To Military and Law enforcement,
putting their lives on the line every day,
while providing an unappreciative
citizenry safety from those who want to
harm us all.

Acknowledgements

Natalie Groshek Staley contributed significant content to this book. Her photography, like the cover, beautifully captures our vibrant world. Enjoy it throughout the manuscript. Natalie's contribution goes far beyond the photography, insisting on proper context, and she is a brutal but loving editor. We have over the years grown as both a photography and writing team.

A Flower for Natalie -Photo -Wayne Staley

Table of Contents

Introduction

I wrote, <u>"The Little Boy Asked Why? The Search for Answers"</u> with the young adults, and our grandchildren, in my mind and heart. They deserve to know how America fell from the greatest economic power in the world, to a country struggling to provide opportunities to a very smart and highly educated populace. They also deserve to know there are viable solutions.

The purpose behind this and all future manuscripts is helping the young adults reach their potential. If they do, the resulting America will be greener, more prosperous, and more equitable than at any time in history. Rebuilding America is the only path to positively resolving the national debt. To get there, all of us will have to exercise bravery and change the course of a run-a-way government that is becoming ever more stifling for entrepreneurs and job formation.

My dear precious young adults, you are the reason we married, raised families, and sacrificed. We want and need you to succeed. You are truly the future for civilized society and the great hope for building a free America for yourselves and future generations.

Make good, well-informed decisions. Do not let anyone steal your future with lies, corruption, misinformation, or coercion. While most people will help, others will use you for their own gain. You must do it for yourselves, and you ARE strong enough to win the fight.

Part One - Why?

1. The Little Boy Asked Why?

While on a research trip to the Gulf of Mexico, I had a strange dream that continues to jolt my consciousness, not hauntingly but as a subtle reminder.

As the dream unfolded, I am riding an ATV on a strange, oil slick, dark road with mud-like, but glassy texture. All structure and life were totally absent until I approached two racially mixed boys, sitting on this strange substance, dressed in patched but spotlessly clean clothes. The oldest, about four, was repairing a nondescript device while the smaller boy, quiet throughout the encounter, played with a broken toy truck.

I asked the older boy, "where is everyone?'

He looked up with the sweetest face, his eyes clear and tearless, answering almost in a whisper, "Gone, they are all gone. There's just me and my brother."

"Where did they go?"

"I don't know."

He returned his attention to the device, than looking up, the serene, inquisitive look still etched in his young face, asked, "Why"?

Desperately searching for an answer, I quietly explained, "Well, hurricane Katrina may have washed everything away."

"No, not that", he replied quietly.

I woke up, struggling for answers, aware the child's question was more profound and inclusive than the response. Unfolding like a sequel, the dream reemerged and focused on the children. Before I could speak, the boy, with face calm and beatific, asked again with infinite patience,

"Why?"

The dream, strange and confused, had two simultaneous endings. First, it faded, and then I simply rode away. The latter ending raised a question - if there was no one to care for them, why had I not taken the boys to safety. Eventually the answer materialized. Imagined into existence, they are home, locked solidly into my heart and conscience, catalysts for inquiry and antidotes for apathy.

As systems analysts, the words, what, why, when, where, and how, are essential fact-finding and problem solving questions. Our mobile technological society is obsessed with "what," searching Google and instantly equating the finding as facts.

The Five Why's is a process improvement concept, introduced by Taiichi Ohno, the master behind the Toyota Production system.

Wikipedia has done a great job of defining the concept.

> The 5 Whys is an iterative question-asking technique used to explore the cause-and-effect relationships underlying a particular problem. The primary goal of the technique is to determine the root cause of a defect or problem. (The "5" in the name derives from an empirical observation on the number of iterations typically required to resolve the problem.) http://en.wikipedia.org/wiki/5_Whys - cite_note-1

Foundational to curiosity, the significant question is to ask why. While obscured, there is always a cause and effect. Questions range from the macro to the minuscule. The answer to a question, such as "why do some individuals find it easy to forfeit their freedoms?" is both complicated and controversial. Some people have reservations about posing contentious questions, while others ask why, seeking clarity, facts, and truth. Without knowledge of the causes for an action/inaction, the effects lack clarity and rationality. Refusing to ask relevant questions measures our fear, not intellectual relevancy, and perpetuates the situation.

Given the challenge from the little boy, what remains is the application of the tools and defining solutions. First, we will state an unequivocal fact and provide the data. The United States is by far the richest, most successful country in the world. We passionately want to perpetuate this success for our children - all of the children.

Following is a partial list of whys, and each reader will expand it with his or her own questions.

- Given the United States is the richest country, why should any citizen be hungry or without healthcare?

- Given the vast resources and state of our nation, why do we not have a collective mission statement?

- Why continue to ignore waste in government and why not hold elected officials accountable?

- Why are we the people fighting with each other instead of against non-responsive, corrupted government officials?

- Americans value honesty and justice, so why not hold our government accountable for its deception and lies? Why does it matter unless we are complicit through apathy or political affiliation?

- Why has fear stilled our voices, and sapped the courage to speak for our children?

- Why, given that Americans spend more for education than any other country, do we rank 17th among the industrialized nations. Only 75% of our students graduate from high school. Source: http://thelearningcurve.pearson.com/the-report/towards-an-index-of-education-outputs

- Why, given the amount of money spent on public education, do students at Catholic schools, receiving zero governmental funding, score consistently 10-20 points higher? Source: The Nations Report Card, Department of Education

- Why do children go to school hungry? Source: http://feedingamerica.org/.

- Why must Title 1 teachers beg for school supplies from their family members? Source: www.wkrn.com/story/21858334/supplieshttp://www.huffingtonpost.com/2012/08/23/survey-many-teachers-repo_n_1822777.html

- Given that pollution is global, why do Americans look the other way as China builds coal power plants, and we dismantle coal production in the United States? Why are their cheap products more important than our environmental values?

The little boys in my dream are an incarnation of our children and grandchildren, who always ask why.

Based on the criteria "is it good for our children," some evaluative questions are required about how well we are achieving this objective.

- Why have we burdened future generations with an ultra expensive healthcare system?

- Why are we allowing our government to erode the very rights our children deserve?

- Why perpetuate an education system teaching our students what to think, instead of how to think?

- Why does our education system leave graduates thousands of dollars in debt?

- Why not re-engineer and address the education system, matching degrees to employer's requirements with an integrated college and technical school system?

- Why are future generations burdened with a national debt, greater than one year of national GDP, requiring them to pay higher interest and taxes for a lifetime?

- Why have we not fixed the social security system, making it available for future generations, instead of subsidizing seniors on the backs of the young?

- Why have we created a business environment where job development is discouraged through governmental regulations, resulting in high unemployment among the young?

- Why are we not creating a society where children can vision big, and then work to make those passions a reality?

- Why have we created a society where, for the first time in American history, the future prospects for our children and grandchildren are less than prior generations?

The dream children permeated my conscience, dramatically escalating the challenge to take action. Society is failing our children, facing futures with reduced opportunities, a remarkable broken continuum. Ask if you are responsible for their future, because if not, their fate is sealed. If yes, take the time to honestly answer these questions, and ask "why" five times to each answer to find the root cause.

The American people differ on questions and answers (solutions), and reflect the disagreement with our divided government. While all are required to fix the problems, there must first be an honest, civil dialogue. Currently, many carefully avoid controversial issues, even among family members. Perhaps all need more courage to ask important questions, hopefully in a non-confrontational way. Nothing positive will result until we bury the conflict between liberals, conservatives, et al, confronting common issues as one people.

Our readers will disagree on cause and effect, options and solutions. These debates are welcome because honest inquiry and dialogue lead to enlightenment and solutions.

I hope we have the guts to face up to the true reasons for the decline of the American system and define the problems. Once defined, ask what actions will fix the problems, than take positive steps to implement solutions. If we care enough, then positive changes will occur, enabling future generations to blossom like flowers on the new tree of opportunity, entrepreneurialism, and prosperity.

2. *Greed Over Common Sense*

Once upon a time in a country named America, times were prosperous. The great conflict, World War II, was in the rear-view mirror and the future was bright and shiny. Every day millions of people, lunch pails in hand, kissed their family members, got into their cars, and drove to high-paying factory jobs. They made every type of product required for their society, and in turn, bought products from other local and national suppliers. The money cycled within the American economic system, and everyone who wanted to work, could find a job. Every manufacturing job generated six to ten other jobs in health care, banking, services, transportation, and synergistic manufacturing.

The government's share of the economy was less than twenty percent of GDP. Regulation was light handed, and entrepreneurship and business startups boomed across the country.

Since there were opportunities of every type, the less affluent did not envy those with money. They worked and studied hard, determined to elevate their own status. America had a thriving middle-class, generated and maintained by a production economy.

Communism reared its ugly head in Europe, and was our biggest enemy. Russia and China embodied the communist empire. For many years, the cold war added to economic wealth as all sides built huge industrial/military complexes, machines of war, and atomic bombs. Each country participated in a surreal game called Mutual Assured Destruction (MAD), where the participants in a nuclear war would annihilate each other. Life in Russia as a peasant was hard, and for those better off, still devoid of personal freedoms.

At its core, communism is about presumed equality, with everyone regardless of status enjoying their share of the economic pie, left over from the elites. If the pie was large, the peasants had a little more. The idea of personal incentive was an alien concept. Based on this premise the following Russian joke was either hilarious or sick, depending on one's perspective, but I will repeat it here for context. I was unable to trace the original author.

> "God came down from heaven and appeared to a Russian peasant, saying, 'You can have anything you want, just ask.' Images of great wealth and personal stature flashed through the peasants' mind. God then delivered the caveat. 'The one condition is that whatever you receive; your neighbor will get twice as much.' The peasant, rethinking, replied, 'Put out one of my eyes."

American exceptionalism prevailed. In a turn-a-round from historic practices, where the victor occupied the vanquished, our factory system rebuilt Germany and Japan. Democracy and freedom really worked, and even the Berlin wall fell, and communism faltered as Russia fell apart.

However, prosperity has a partner named greed, and as American prosperity grew, so did the greed. The rich wanted more wealth, (we all did), and government wanted more power and control. Each segment set out to acquire those objectives. Government passed regulations, used by businesses as an excuse to move jobs off shore. People loved big government while hating business. They forgot the lessons learned from communism/socialism and the common sense of free enterprise. Prosperity suffered. Government ballooned to twenty-five percent of GDP, taking productive capital out of the economy.

On a family trip, we developed a frequently used descriptive phase,

"Greed over common-sense" and unfortunately, this concept became the modus operandi for business and government.

Downsizing and redistribution, the forces that changed America, were processes not an event. It took less than thirty years to reduce the greatest nation on earth to one struggling in the world economy. In context of historical time, it was/is an explosive event.

The economic destruction resulted from internal greed, not nuclear bombs. Forgotten is the lesson that work and production generate wealth, and without wealth, there is nothing to redistribute. We bought into the intense, but fuzzy concept of income inequality, regardless of citizen's level of contribution, personal responsibility, or the economic consequences.

The great thing about prosperity is that it is fungible and exchangeable, and we are still the greatest country in the world in terms of resources and freedoms. We need to stop fighting among ourselves, and recognize that prosperity is the path to resolving many of our social ills.

It means rediscovering a basic truth; prosperity results from circulating wealth within our own economic system. By responsibly using our natural resources and freeing ingenuity, our economy has the capacity to provide opportunities to every citizen. We can start by expanding our manufacturing capacity instead of transferring it to China and Mexico. Although robots replaced many production jobs, it still requires the creation of jobs servicing these industries and society in general.

There are two missing ingredients. They are effective leadership and the lack of a national mission. Wandering around aimlessly will not strengthen America, but perpetuate bleeding prosperity and expose us to the predatory actions of Russia, China, and ISIS.

3. Why the Redistribution of America

Painting-Wayne Staley

"The <u>power</u> of population is indefinitely greater than the <u>power</u> in the <u>earth</u> to produce subsistence for man" - Thomas Robert <u>Malthus</u>.

Population vs. Resources

Malthus' book fueled a debate that rages to this date. Is the world running out of food and other resources because of population growth?

The three featured works that are foundational to the environmental movement are <u>An Essay on the Principle of Population, The Limits to Growth – A Report for the Club of Rome's Project on the Predicament of Mankind, and Silent Spring.</u>

These first two documents address the relationships and consequences between natural and human systems.

<u>An Essay on the Principle of Population,</u> by Malthus, published in 1798, established the framework of dependency between population and resources.

Malthus performed an evaluation of future resource availability based on then known reserves, consumption, circumstances, and population growth. Essentially, he wanted to know how long resources would last given the rate of consumption per human being and the availability of resources (capital). <u>The Limits to Growth</u> expanded the logic.

For Malthus, the relationship between population growth (independent component) and resource limits (dependent) drove the investigation and essay. It is Malthus' contention, and one adopted by subsequent studies, that population growth is exponential, that is "2, 4, 8, 16," while the rate of increased resource availability, or production, is linear, or "1, 2, 3,4." The speed of technological development is putting the premise in question.

The consequences are obvious. That is, consumption will eventually exceed finite production and resources will run out. Following is the method and logic.

If each person consumes an average of two pounds of food per day, one billion people require two billion pounds of food. This calculation is linear but food consumption is not (linear vs. exponential). Those in the developed countries overindulge as half the world searches for food.

Capital plays a role. Those with wealth or access to capital hoard the resources, taking a proportionately greater share to distribute among themselves while dividing the smaller portion among the larger, less wealthy populations. This effect is worldwide as investors and the wealthy gain from an expanding stock market while the middle and less affluent classes lose income and purchasing power.

As the growth rate of the undeveloped countries increase, the consumption of food per individual may stay the same but the total consumption of food increases in direct relationship to the population. As undeveloped countries increase their standard of living and approach the consumption level of the industrialized world, food requirements will multiply due to the increased demand. Eventually, demand may outstrip supply.

Self-actualization
Personal growth fulfillment
Consumption decreases may occur

Esteem Needs
Personal and work achievement, status, responsibility, reputation
Larger dwellings, cars, travel options, greater consumption

Belonging and love needs
Family, affection, relationships, work groups, cities, national identity
Family, housing, travel, education, consumptive, automation

Safety needs
Shelter, Security, social order, laws, parameters, stability, medical
Tribal, more advanced tools

Biological and Physiological Needs
Survival needs – air, food, drink, shelter, warmth, sex, sleep
Basic tools

Greater resource usage

Greater Impact on Ecosystems

Based on Maslow's Hierarchy of Needs
(original five-stage model)

The availability of resources is a function of scarcity and price. Those in the developed world, with greater access to capital, will maintain consumption levels at the expense of those financially troubled countries. In this way, capital helps to restore equilibrium and balance between supply and demand. It does not restore parity of access to resources. Supply will control the population as it does in many other animal species, and given a shortage of food, people will die of starvation. The effect is a reduction of population to sustainable levels.

While criticized in some quarters, the methods used by Malthus were valid. The flaws were the same ones encountered by many models, past and present. These are the availability of irrefutable, accurate, detailed information on specific resources and the ability to quantify the potential, timing, and effects of technology.

Unlike Malthus, we have computers that can recalculate every variable in seconds. Without proper data on each variable, conclusions calculated in nano-seconds still generate contentious conclusions. The model Malthus employed passed the logic of reasonableness.

The purpose behind Malthus' study is questionable, given that he was an elitist living in England when the slave trade was at its peak, and black and poor people had lower value in that society. His concern was the rapid growth rate of the working class/low-income groups with an accompanying increase in resource competition. It was the beginning of the industrial age. Eli Whitney had developed the cotton gin only five years prior, and the steamboat was a future event. Malthus wanted to determine if there would be enough resources to perpetuate the high standard of living enjoyed by the elite of the day and if not he advocated war, pestilence and other population control devices.

The Limits to Growth, the second, and for our purposes, more significant of the two studies on population and resources was written in 1972 by MIT Project Team authors Donella H. Meadows, Dennis L. Meadows, Jorgen Randers, and William W. Behrens III, and sponsored by The Club of Rome.

While there were numerous studies by a wide range of authors discussing the dependent population/resource relationship, such as in the book Peak Oil, (events proved this theory wrong), any serious study on the topic referenced or led to The Limits to Growth as the source document. It established a paradigm of intellectual thought and was foundational to the environmental movement. Its concepts are pervasive in the world's culture but often operate in the background or as a part of other social philosophies.

The Limits to Growth struck the chords of a world sick of the Vietnam War and reeling from the freedom movement in the sixties. America was primed for a world cause. China had yet to start its journey into the industrialized world. Computers were still novelties in the workplace.

The study contained research into five specific areas, per the Table of Contents:

- The Nature of Exponential Growth
- The Limits of Exponential Growth
- Growth in the World System
- Technology and the Limits of Growth
- The State of Global Equilibrium

There is not a specific chapter devoted to the topic of the environment, but the environment forms a pervasive thread throughout the work.

The book takes the concepts introduced by Malthus and expands them in relationship to population, finite resources, and sophistication of analytics. The analysts created an early computer model, a fact criticized by those unfamiliar with the power of either modeling or computers. The systems approach was classic and the scientific method impeccably observed. A valid model was carefully constructed, and dependencies, calculations, inputs, outputs, assumptions, and conclusions, clearly documented.

The most significant focal point was over-reach, consuming resources at a rate greater than replenishment, or replaced by substitutes. The question, were resources sustainable at a predictable rate? Using weighting factors significantly changed the resulting calculation but the projected consequence is a function of time, not probability.

The study is sobering. It leaves little doubt that if population grows without restriction, whether resource usage is linear or exponential, we

14

will run out of limited resources in less than one hundred years. The question is which ones, and is technology capable of creating timely substitutes?

Expanding populations in the developing countries translates into more people attempting to climb the ladder of Maslow's Hierarchy of Needs. Economic expansion accelerated as China and other emerging markets became more industrialized. According to scientists, the exponential consumption of resources is a reality.

Pollution

The Limits to Growth addresses pollution of the biosphere in strong terms. To project the effects of pollution, the authors assigned dependent values to the causes of pollution. This enabled calculations of the projected environmental effects based on resource use and population. They state, "We have almost no knowledge about where the upper limits to these pollution curves might be," meaning they lacked specific knowledge of the effect of resources on the climate, and therefore, the calculated results were relative, not absolute.

The researchers meticulously acknowledged shortfalls in data detail. Many readers ignored the caveat of "the best available" and used the report and formulas to support conclusions of their own (then and now), in absolute interpretations. History has proven most of these were invalid premises, yet decisions with historic consequences were based on these assumptions.

Study recommendations

One key point was that countries should shift from industrial activity to service and health care sectors, thereby avoiding pollution from production. This had profound and far-reaching effects.

Many entities, including business and government, were excited about this new direction, ignoring the recommendation from the report that America downsize, (my word, not theirs), until it reached economic parity with the rest of the world.

Business, on the lookout for cheaper production sources, dismantled vertical factories, which performed all the work from foundry through assembly, for core competency, farming out operations to companies that performed them at a lower cost. This horizontal factory system eventually made it easier to offshore operations.

A clean environment became one of society's stated primary priorities, rightly so given disasters like Love Canal, an industrial chemical waste site. The passage of harsh environmental regulations provided industry with the incentive to relocate manufacturing to Mexico, through NAFTA, and pollute with impunity, then to China and other developing nations. Manufacturing jobs in America dropped from twenty-five percent of the work force to twelve.

The emergence of the projected solution, an intellectually driven service state, failed to materialize. All global boundaries disappeared with the internet, allowing instant transmission of information and intellectual property across the globe. Technology, the most underestimated component in the studies, destroyed the dream of a giant, vibrant super-service economy before it even left the incubator.

The Limits to Growth provides important insights and relationships into key environmental and social issues. On page 93, the authors disavow any intent at prediction:

> "These graphs are not exact predictions of the value of the variables at any particular year in the future. They are indications of the system's behavioral tendencies only."

While the stated intent was not to make predictions, the methodology itself forces conclusions. All forecasts and predictions are wrong to some degree. Decisions based on data of this type are only as precise as the data, selection of formulas and the methodology.

The authors make a series of recommendations aimed at eco-equilibrium. These include steps to maintain population, resources, and production (capital) in equilibrium, sustaining environmental integrity and conserving resources. The objective was to define methods to delay the effects to the "limits to growth" identified in the study.

These recommendations contain a series of rules governing all human activity. While the book does not specifically recommend a world government, it would be impossible to achieve the objectives without a utopian perspective and a benign authoritarian global government.

Preceding this recommendation, the authors questioned the ability of government to deal with the complexities and variables indicated by the model. It has been my experience that government manages resources poorly. Two quick examples are the U.S. Postal Service and the Veterans Health Care system.

The study proposes the following found on page 171 in <u>The Limits to Growth</u>:

> "The capital plant and the population are constant in size."

The birth rate equals the death rate and the capital investment rate equals the depreciation rate.

Based on this recommendation, control of population, the highest priority, translates into reducing birthrates to match death rates or increasing death rates to match birth rates. Freezing population levels below capital growth and resource usage achieves equilibrium.

One of the tenets is abortion and birth control. While not specifically mentioned, euthanasia is another tool for population control. Part of the phrasing "elimination of unwanted children" provides an answer. If birth control, abstinence, and a higher death rate achieve zero population growth, fewer abortions are required. The reality is that zero growth is difficult to achieve without abortions, a lot of them and euthanasia, a lot of it. The problem is that abortion and euthanasia are murder, and a highly divisive social issue.

The best tool for controlling population is through the health care system. Not coincidentally, the first agenda item for the Obama administration was the Affordable Health Care Act. Coupling the ACA to the Department of Revenue establishes a National Database of You and Me. President Obama's actions have been devastating for African-American families, as they lose power through demographic change, neglect, low population growth, non-competitive education levels, and the effects of abortion. President Obama has been actively bringing in immigrants and rapidly increasing the Muslim population, thereby creating severe job competition for black Americans. No president in modern history has done more to destroy a demographic than Obama has with the Black community.

While researching this topic, no one could state the issue more clearly than J. Kenneth Blackwell, Aborting black America, The 'black lives matter' slogan excludes the unborn.

> Legalized abortion is working out exactly as Margaret
> Sanger intended. Sanger, the founder of the nation's
> largest abortion provider, Planned Parenthood, was
> part of the eugenics movement back in the 1930s. Her
> goal was to use abortion to cull what she considered
> inferior races from the human gene pool. According to
> Sanger, "Colored people are like human weeds and are

to be exterminated." She opened her first abortion clinics in inner cities, and it's no accident that even today, "79 percent of Planned Parenthood's abortion facilities are located in black or minority neighborhoods."

http://www.washingtontimes.com/news/2015/jan/21/j-kenneth-blackwell-black-abortions-a-crisis-in-am/

In time, the government will have the capacity, if not the moral authority or support of the people, to ration healthcare as a tool to control population. Obviously, this means the American populace, not the world in general, will continue to pay the price for population control, making more room for immigrants in the United States.

The widening chasm between economic demographics carries an implicit level of health care affordability that may translate into the longer life spans for the rich and shorter for the poor. Sadly, this may be the de facto implementation of population control.

Equally important is a zero growth, zero sum economy, which allows central control, under the socialism label, and prevents the over-reach of resource utilization. The authors identify the United States as one country whose standard of living requires a reduction to achieve and maintain global equilibrium.

> "We unequivocally support the contention that a brake imposed on demographic and economic spirals must not lead to a freezing of the status quo of economic development of the world's nations. (Pg. 198). If such a proposal were advanced by the rich nations, it would be taken as a final act of neocolonialism. The achievement of a harmonious state of global economic, social, and ecological equilibrium must be a joint venture based on joint

conviction, with benefits for all. The greatest leadership will be demanded from the economically developed countries, *for the first step towards such a goal would be for them to encourage deceleration in the growth of their own material output while, at the same time, assisting the developing nations in their efforts to advance their economies more rapidly*". <u>The Limits to Growth</u>

That is exactly what President Obama has done.

Over-reach is not preventable unless every country buys off and complies with the agreement. Taking actions unilaterally, as Obama has in America, will not achieve global equilibrium. It will only destroy America. Who in America specifically voted to downsize our economy and give away our future? By definition, preventing over-reach has a profound effect on economies, commodities, consumerism, travel, and recreation, with freedoms replaced by dystopia.

> "All input and output rates – births, deaths, investment, and depreciation-are kept to a minimum."

This requires strict governmental control preferably at a global level. On one hand it supports the rights of choice but on the other takes them away. China provides a hard example, when the government encouraged rapid population growth, then attempted to limit the consequences by imposing a "one child per family" rule.

> "The levels of capital and population and the ratio of the two are set in accordance with the values of society."

Managing capital and population in accordance with the values of society allows the government tight control over the means of production, pollution, land use, energy usage, and any activity that would upset the environmental equilibrium. The question is who establishes the values? (See the chapter on "Trust.")

Compliance with the recommendations could default into tyranny, resolving one problem but creating a worse one. Is dystopian life worth living? Does it save our species while destroying our humanity?

Theories for reducing population emerged as environmentalists adopted the concepts of the report. The mantra became "zero population growth," with abortion, birth control, and sex education as the primary weapons. The industrialized countries cut birthrates but the emerging countries did not, opening the way for large migrations of legal and illegal immigrants from the poor countries into the industrialized ones. The consequences are still ongoing, and most are proving to be detrimental to free societies.

There were two sequels to The Limits to Growth. The latest is Limits to Growth, The 40 Year Update.

The Limits to Growth proved to be accurate in many ways based on given scientific data. The most noteworthy issues were global warming and over-reach. There is every reason to believe that over-reach has been significant and will probably increase in the future unless factors slow it down.

The conclusion remains that current levels of consumption and production are not sustainable, and that the world will experience resource shortages. The last report, none-the-less, is optimistic if we are wise enough to take the appropriate actions.

Issues with the report

The problem is that discredited and inaccurate data on global warming and population raise questions about the contents of the work. Surprisingly, much of the rhetoric about the environment is immaterial.

Instead of talking about it, we need to take real actions to be environmental stewards.

The word "finite" means "limited" but it does not imply knowledge of what those limitations are. The limits are very complicated to quantify in highly complex systems because of the extreme number of variables. Given incomplete data, calculating precise conclusions is difficult. The authors of The Limits to Growth make this point clear and their generalized conclusions are proving correct. We know, for example, that eventually consumption will reach and exceed capacity. Essential resources will run out unevenly and will influence the rates of production or use of other resources. We do not know if technology will advance fast enough to solve the potential shortage of critical materials.

Given the numerous unquantifiable variables, it is difficult to calculate the rate of discoveries in innovation and technology, but we do have an insight. In 1965, Intel co-founder Gordon Moore stated, "The number of transistors incorporated in a chip will approximately double every 24 months." This was "Moore's Law." The computer chip changed everything, moving computer technology, and perhaps other applied sciences, from linear to exponential growth.

Convergence

President Barack Obama was born on August 4, 1961, and was a student in high school and college when the great American outsourcing of jobs began. By then, the universities fully embraced the environmental movement. We know little of his background relative to environmentalism but as a Senator and President, he aligned with the extreme elements of the movement.

Writing his first book, The Audacity of Hope: Thoughts on Reclaiming the American Dream, President Obama makes his ideology very clear. America is guilty of neo-colonialism, and much of our wealth was ill earned on the backs of slaves and the developing nations. His presidency has been a work-in-progress to rectify all of these perceived injustices. Given the Law of Unintended Consequences, he created additional layers of injustice against the American people, mostly against those he pretended to champion.

Throughout history, disparate ideals converge, retaining their respective paradigms, but creating intense energy for change. Environmentalism and Obama are uneasy partners in a net sum game where the total resource consumption and capital must remain in equilibrium to achieve sustainability. While environmentalism is concerned about the overall concept of resource conservancy, Obama is committed to an ideology obsessed with how wealth and resources are distributed, who gets what, and who participates in the rewards.

Redistribution means to "divide something among a group in a different way." (Merriam-Webster.) The word gained attention in 2008 when Barack Obama, as a candidate for President of the United States, inadvertently used the term during a discussion with Joe the Plumber.

There was an immediate uproar. The candidate was proposing a socialist concept, the Robin Hood syndrome, where one robs from the rich and gives to the poor. It was hyperbole, distracting from an intelligent search within the meaning of the phrase, preventing discovery of the consequences behind the concept. Had voters spent less time reacting and more time analyzing, they might have discovered what Obama meant when he promised to "fundamentally change America" through redistribution and downsizing. Had they understood it would be at the expense of the middle class and already economically challenged minorities, the outcome may have been different.

Examples of redistribution occur everywhere. Parents paying for college, and contributions to church and other charitable donations are redistribution of wealth. Everyone agrees this is proper because it is entirely a matter of personal choice.

The traditional American concept of redistribution is equality, which requires taking more from the rich to make sure other people have shelter, food, clothing, health care, and educational opportunities.

This concept extends to other humanitarian activities. We all want to use some of our resources to help others in the global community. This raises a difficult question. How much is a "fair share" and how high is the price society must pay to help others throughout the world? What costs are incurred at the expense of our current economy? How will this attempt at parity affect those citizens trapped by a changing workplace? What happens to the future prospects of our younger generations?

Obama's concept of redistribution extends far beyond the rich sharing more with the poor. His vision is redistributing wealth to the third world while downsizing America in the world economy and as a super-power.

While one could say that he had never stated this purpose, his actions make the objective very clear. Much of what he wanted to accomplish is completed. We are a weaker country; our economy has deteriorated, and we have lost status and trust in the global hierarchy. Some people question whether he understands the consequences of these objectives on America and the world. Without question - he does. Even more troubling, do the citizens of America comprehend the multitude of ways the completion of Obama's dream changed the way we live and the world our children and grandchildren will inherit.

Government is involved in redistributing revenues gained through taxation and fees that pay for services demanded by law or the population. The problem occurs when government redistributes without authorization from the constituency or for purposes of which we do not approve. It is progressivism on steroids, expediently acquiring higher levels of central control. No one has the legal power to "rob the rich and give to everyone else," accept Congress. Redistribution, when interpreted as free stuff, is delusional, because everyone affected pays higher taxes, while suffering from the loss of investment potential and reduced opportunities. In reality, the rich are never taxed more, because they can afford lawyers and tax accountants. The middle and lower classes <u>always</u> absorb the higher cost of redistribution.

Redistribution as practiced by President Obama is a net sum game where total resources stagnate because of low economic growth. Control over those resources is reserved and used to retain wealth and power. The populace gets poorer. Economic data proves the point.

The McKinsey Global Institute published a report titled,

The death of the middle class is worse than you think

https://www.msn.com/en-us/money/markets/the-death-of-the-middle-class-is-worse-than-you-think/ar-BBujiY4?ocid=spartandhp

> A new report from the McKinsey Global Institute, with the chilling title "Poorer than their Parents: Flat or Falling Incomes in Advanced Economies," shows just why this is the case. According to the paper, the trend in stagnating or declining incomes for middle-class workers is not just confined to the United States but is a

global phenomenon hurting workers across the wealthy world.

One quote summarizes the document.

> *To put it bluntly: A huge swath of the world's population, one that had been taught to expect their material wealth to grow through their lifetimes and across generations, has learned that this promise was a lie. No wonder voters in the rich world <u>are being seduced</u> by radical politics and specious solutions to their economic problems.*

If the entire world is involved in a net sum game, global resource utilization remains the same, but both consumption and production move from one location to another. Wealth and power move in relationship, often gradually. China practices growth concepts, and is gaining economic strength and power at our expense.

Consequences

Money moves globally, and capital will grow somewhere regardless of the amount redistributed. Our national debt is $19.3 trillion dollars, while our annual GDP is $18 trillion (<u>http://www.multpl.com/us-gdp-inflation-adjusted/table</u>).

We must break the net-sum game by growing the economy, and progressivism (socialism) will not get the job done.

The two most significant policies leading to equilibrium are population and controlling the means of production and distribution. The solution itself calls for a radical reduction in manufacturing, which drives wealth creation. Cutting production, in turn, reduces economic strength and the ability to deal with environmental issues.

In extreme environmentalism, both production and consumption shrink to fit the capability of the planet to provide resources (equilibrium) while retaining sustainability. In this case, the net sum game is not applicable because environmentalism demands a significant reduction in the size of the pie, or the total resources used. Given this scenario, there will be winners and a greater number of losers. The United States has and will continue to suffer substantial wealth degeneration, and be unable to create jobs. We have high debt with inadequate investment and incentive to sustain the nation's wealth.

As our economy falters or is permanently weakened, the environmental standards will collapse. Rich nations can afford new laws, but the environment suffers when wealth formation is restricted. In a controlled dystopian society, resources and wealth migrate to the elite, and everyone else gets the leftovers. If nothing is left, nature serves to constrain distribution. Given the massive redistribution currently in progress in the United States, we will unilaterally reduce our standards. Allowing ourselves to enter a state of economic free fall increases the risk becoming a third-world country.

http://competitiveamerica.us/ we make the following observation.

> When economies collapse, the net sum game is operational, and necessity trumps basic environmental preservation. Americans foolishly believe it could never happen here.

> Look around at the empty factories. Drive through the inner cities (like that of Detroit). Serve at a food kitchen and see how people live without jobs. Afterward, listen to the rhetoric about how things are getting better. Think about political correctness. Consider the constant reshaping and programming that result from a corrupted political process, press and education systems.

Ask why our factory jobs have fled the country. Ask why the greatest country ever on this planet is unable to generate jobs, educate its people, preserve its environment, and lead the way to a higher human state.

Study the histories of Venezuela, Argentina, and Brazil.

Effect

The industrialized civilizations are working hard to save our environment. The Western civilizations, Europe, Canada, and the United States, have practiced the principle of zero population growth, and severely reduced greenhouse gasses. While feel good achievements, we have launched potential long-term consequences.

The most severe price, in the United States, was GIVING AWAY our manufacturing base - the core job generator and economic engine for our country. The second is creating a population void, being filled by immigrants from countries with unchecked population growth.

Environment

Most of the world, including China, has lesser concern for the environment, trading it for economic advantage, or are unable to invest in the technologies and clean-up efforts.

Increasingly tighter EPA regulations cause the continued transfer of jobs to foreign competitors. One of the major premises for increased environmental regulation is Global warming. It is useful to test the premise and examine the consequences of incompletely stating and understanding issues.

The truth about GHG and manufacturing

China surged past the United States in industrial output. The following chart shows Green House Gas (GHG) emissions and industrial output in relation to country and equivalent pollution ratios.

	China	USA
GHG Emissions	9679.30	6668.79
Industrial Output (Trillion$)	2.9	2.43
Industrial Output %	54.4	45.6
Greenhouse Gas %	59.2	40.8
Ratio	1.17	.89

The last line shows the ratio of pollution percentages vs. manufacturing output in total between the two countries. The ratio of GHG emissions per volume is much lower for the United States than for China.

Assume the green house gas (GHG) scenario is correct. If Americans cut GHG emissions to zero tomorrow, and everyone moves into caves and tepees, it would make little difference. **China will increase emissions by a factor of three before 2030, making the worst-case GHG scenario a reality.**

This data is from the environmental agreement the Obama administration signed with China. It also requires America to cut another 26% of our emissions, meaning more American jobs and opportunities will disappear.

If there is true global climate destruction, as most believe, where is the international anger? Politicians, academia, and environmental activists from every country should be screaming to punish China and other international polluters by not purchasing their products. There is no outcry. Instead, we reward polluters by tightening our regulations and outsourcing even more high-paid jobs. The key question: Do we destroy America's economic future in a meaningless quest to compensate for the rest of the world? **I call this madness.**

Environmental imperatives

Assume that greenhouse warming is a hoax. Acid rain, polluted water, and finite hydrocarbons are <u>real</u> and <u>tangible</u>. We must respect Planet Earth or risk passing a diminished world to future generations. Plentiful American hydrocarbons are a bridge to the future, one with global implications. We must develop energy alternates but do so with complete situational knowledge allowing strategic evaluation and the development of practical tactics. Stated differently, science leads, not government.

The greatest force to achieve this new reality lies in America, powered by the intellectual power of the young adults. Building a green industrial system in America and shutting down pollution from both China and Mexico is a noble and achievable cause. To realize this objective requires both courage and commitment, by the people and the governments.

Population

Western civilization adopted the principles of extreme environmentalism to control population. The balance of the world did not. This created a void, and immigrants from third-world countries who do not share Western values, flooded into the space. Eventually, those populations may become the majority.

The United States will be a plurality. Latinos are currently the fastest-growing minority, but Muslim immigration, by the sheer strength of numbers, will become extremely significant.

The group with the most to lose, by continuing on the present social path, is the black communities. Their population will shrink as a percent of the total, and their voting power will dissipate. They are and will be the great loser in the demographic war. These are the reasons, regardless of promises, that politicians will continue to ignore their needs.

These same forces will eventually affect racial demographics, and then religious philosophies.

Immigration, and its impact, are a work in process, as discussed in the chapters titled, "Our Immigrant Roots," and "The Children Immigrants."

In the final analysis, we are not saving the environment, but destroying America, as we know it.

4. Economic facts

This chapter is based on real time data. To make it easy for fact-checkers, the figures used are from two sources, http://www.usdebtclock.org/, and https://research.stlouisfed.org/fred2/series/USGOVT .

On the day of this writing,

- Employment numbers show government workers at 23.8 million versus 20.7 Million in 2000, an increase of 3.1 million. It has increased by 200,000 in the last five months in spite of the slow economy.

- Manufacturing employees 12.397 million versus 19.3 million in 2000, a reduction of 6.9 million jobs in the last fifteen years. In the last five months, 103,000 manufacturing jobs have been lost.

- Facts: In the last five months, Government added 200,000 while manufacturing lost 103,000. Government is now twice as large as our manufacturing sector. While manufacturing generates wealth, government spends it.

- Our national debt is $19.3 trillion dollars. In 2000, the debt was $5.7 trillion, an increase of $13.6 trillion.

- Every citizen of American now owes $59,534.

- Taxpayer debt per person is $160,158.

- Student loan debt 1.346 trillion dollars.

- The gross national product is 18.3 trillion, and the national debt exceeds one year of GDP.

- This year, we paid 2.410 trillion in interest on the debt. If interest rates increase, so will the interest on our national debt.

- Our spending is 35% greater than income.

- If big government is broke, and the 35% rate clearly proves it is, how can it provide more services and freebies?

The answer is obvious, our broke government is taking more of the productive money out of the economy, and spending it on non-productive government services that get politicians re-elected. Capital investment has dried up, and the number of small business startups (which generates most of the jobs) has dropped substantially.

Without capital investment, the economy is shrinking, and so are the jobs and opportunities. At some point, the transfer of wealth from the private to the public sector becomes unsustainable.

Student debt will eventually require repayment, falling on the taxpayers of America, much like the housing crash of 2008.

Infrastructure expenditures this year hit a 30-year low. We have paid 2.4 trillion interest on our 19.3 trillion dollar National Debt, enough money to rebuild all of our infrastructure, and create millions of jobs.

Summary

Never, in the history of humankind has any nation freely given away, and destroyed a major component of its wealth generation, receiving little in return. For humans, fifty years is a long time, but brief in the rise and fall of nations. America has gone from the most prosperous nation on earth to a nation teetering on the edge of financial mediocrity.

5. The Digital Disruption

Disruptive change

Transformation travels at different speeds and levels of intensity, slowly, over a lifetime, or suddenly, in a heartbeat. The use of information, automation, and robotics technology exploded globally, resulting in a massive but still growing digitally driven disruption and reordering.

The concept of disruptive change is destruction and transformation. This reordering results in new paradigms of work and society, creating dynamic opportunities and risks. It introduces chaos into future events. Everyone affected by the new continuum must choose between meeting the challenges or living with the consequences of inaction.

People need courage, awareness, and flexibility when swept up in a reordering. Degrees and jobs, once stable, become obsolete, requiring continual self-reinvention and entrepreneurship.

In turn, a changing world generates alternative opportunities. To succeed, people need to understand and embrace the new rules imposed by technology and globalization, and learn to anticipate the consequences of dramatic change as it affects them.

With shifting and dangerous situations, the ability to make good decisions is the single greatest factor defining success and failure.

The attributes associated with responsible decisions are intellect, reasoning, attitude, personal and social values, adaptability, knowledge, and the ability to anticipate probable results. We are accountable for our decisions and actions, and how they affect our future. Blaming others for our mistakes soothes egos, but is self-defeating.

Social value system

Disruption, triggered by technology and social change, is significantly modifying traditional value systems. Old and New Testament values give way to secular ethics, such as "political correctness," or "for the greater good." Declining values of honesty and transparency are replaced by "Any means justifies the end." To make future decisions about their future, people must understand the hidden agendas behind these terms.

The changing workplace is creating a system split by levels of income and education. A knowledge driven society demands higher education and provides a proportionate rate of compensation. In broad terms, the rich and educated are getting richer. The middle class is collapsing across the full spectrum, and the less educated are getting poorer. Poverty is the fastest growing demographic.

Education has always divided society, providing persons that spend the time, money, and effort acquiring a degree, with much greater job prospects. The factory system had provided opportunities to less-educated workers, and high-paying factory jobs created a middle class. With those jobs gone, the divide between the educated and non-educated has worsened considerably.

Globalization

Globalization and digital technology are the new commercial paradigms. They broke the chain of prosperity for those middle-class persons with limited education and outdated degrees.

In the old industrial world, there were parallel, but linear paths to wealth. A person graduated from high school, went to college, or found a high-paying factory or construction job. Over the last twenty-five years, America exported significant percentages of its manufacturing base and associated jobs to foreign competitors.

These disruptive forces merged and converted our national economy from a production to a consumer-based model. The result of this disruption and its total effect on everyone is unknown but not predestined. We are still the masters of our fate, determined by our decisions and actions. We can ride the waves of change, swim, or drown as the currents sweep us under.

Information processing

Information technologies, specifically computers and smart phones, allow us to access unlimited amounts of information. Abundant research material and knowledge are available, providing multiple methods and opportunities to study scholarly and technical material for source confirmation.

Technology pushes our ability to deal with changing situations while increasing our dependence on devices. Fact checking is fast and easy but search engines record our footprints and lead us to information that reinforces our personal bias. For these reasons, there is frequently a false sense about performing the due diligence needed for good decision-making.

The government and the press collude to feed us biased information. Read the chapter, *The Press*, to find out exactly how they sold a gullible public on the Iran agreement.

Automation

The use of automation, including robots, is rapidly proliferating throughout industry. Of greater importance is the use of highly sophisticated artificial intelligence (AI) applications, providing the functionality to perform professional jobs based on rules and facts.

Digital disruption and jobs

The social, political, and technological upheaval will affect everyone, and as we state in "Decision-making in a Disruptive Reordering," everyone must adjust to the new realities or sink into the waves.

Part Two - Who is Hurt?

6. Generation X

Generation X are the children of the Silent's and the Boomers. Our children belong to this demographic. All have college degrees, are in original marriages, and we are very proud of them. They have, and are, doing an amazing job of raising and educating their children, the Millennials and the Gen Z, preparing them to participate in a complicated and very competitive world. Like every demographic, there are degrees of success and all will not profit equally. Education, for the most part, is the first success factor, but hard work and sound judgment are co-equal.

To understand Generation X, it is useful to redefine earlier groups. The baby-boomers classification covers multiple social iterations, starting in 1946 and ending in 1964, two vastly different worlds. This is very important. The parents of the early Generation X, the Silent Generation, born before or during World War II, were more traditional, and grew-up in two-parent environments. The Baby boomers, parents of the majority of generation X are products of the nineteen-sixties, a very different society. They grew up in the Age of Aquarius, a time of social and sexual revolution rejecting the establishment. While only a small number of people actively participated in events, like Woodstock in 1969, society in general grew far more liberal and supportive of progressive ideals.

Social conflicts erupted throughout the 1950-70 period. In the late nineteen-fifties, the civil rights movement was in full force. The Vietnam War brought violent protests across the country, and civilians spat upon and vilified returning veterans. At Kent State University, students were shot and killed. These events dramatically altered attitudes about free sex, drug use, religion, government, family composition, education, and work. These were among the many challenges Generation X had to face.

The nineteen-sixties signaled the start of the computer age, with the first personal computers in 1981. Generation X, and to a lesser extent society in general, had to assimilate a disruptive technology that eventually changed the workplace, and then all of society. The computer, coupled with the Internet, changed what and how people, live, learn, communicate and interact.

Generation X suffered through a series of social upheavals, but the worst situation was/is economic. The transfer of jobs from the United States to global competitors started just as Generation X students were entering college. The nature and type of jobs changed as Generation X aged. Two-thirds of the factory jobs disappeared, and white-collar, high-tech jobs quickly followed production overseas.

The downsizing of the factory system to foreign competitors occurred on the timelines of the Silent and Boomer generations. Where one parent had been able to support a family, it required two working people. The latchkey child came into being. The downsizing was underway before Generation X finished college. Outsourcing was an accepted business practice, by the time they matured and occupied executive positions. The drift towards socialism, often embraced by the Boomers in the sixties, continues today, with conflicts between free-

40

market capitalism, big-government socialism, and the loss of individualism.

Automation and globalization, coupled with greed, powered the economic change. Government regulations were largely responsible for redistributing America. Generation X apparently perceives redistribution as equality. I view it as degrading America's ability to compete and believe history will reflect badly on some of Generation X's admirable but misguided social attitudes. The reality is that without a wealth generating economy, there will be fewer resources to redistribute, and diminished job opportunities.

In searching through the literature, some writers have problems describing Generation X. I believe they are resilient, adaptive, and survivors. Given the experiences of their generation, dealing with constant change and social turmoil, they were/are very protective toward their children, the Millennials, and Gen Z.

Generation X, heavily influenced by the environmental movement, became the keepers of Mother Earth, and the proponents of nearly all green technologies. I agree with them, but our long-term solutions are markedly different.

I believe America must reindustrialize using every green technology available. Manufacturing is not an excuse to pollute, as occurred in the Second Industrial Revolution. I think the options are clear. Rebuild America or slowly cede our country to China, the least environmentally friendly country on earth.

Generation X needs to re-examine the political, social, and moral circumstances that are downsizing our economy. Without a rebirth of the American dream, the children of Gen X, the Millennials, will face bleak future prospects.

7. The Millennials-America's Future

I have an affinity for the demographic group labeled "Millennials," Generation Y, or Echo Boomers, and extending through Generation Z. A more inclusive label is young adults. Although our grandchildren fit within these categories, the identity goes deeper, and for good reasons. In many ways, we share the same values, but they are the face of the future.

Graduation Day - Photograph-Wayne Staley

Previous generations really stuck it t+o the young adults. Their idealism, unfortunately, exacerbated the situation. Following is a situational summary, and why older generations owe them big time.

The legacy they inherited

We, their elders, shipped American industry offshore. In less than twenty years, America shifted from a production to a consumer based society and we gave away our economic engine.

Under the Bush administration, the national debt ballooned to 4.9 trillion dollars. In 2008, the economy, under extreme stress from personnel debt, and fraudulent investment practices, collapsed into an economic recession. Since 1929-33, other recessions were deeper, but governmental actions prolonged this one for a record seven years. The young adults grew up during this turbulent time.

How the young adults exacerbated the problem

Young people are always impressionable and open. The current education system has programmed a line of thinking that makes them vulnerable to manipulation. They trusted the very people that exploited them, took actions based on these factors, and negatively affected their own prospects, in political, academic, and social situations.

Political

The first mistake was idealistically backing President Obama. In 2012, he won them over by promise and social manipulation. They responded by voting for him 69 to 39 percent, assuring his reelection. In return, the Obama administration stacked the deck against this demographic. There is not enough space in this newsletter to detail all the ways he threw them under the bus, but here are some examples.

President Obama has more than doubled the national debt. Repayment will explode directly on these demographics and their families. It is a poor prognosis for their eventual retirement opportunities.

Given the job situation, young adults find it difficult to buy health care insurance, as mandated by the Affordable Care Art. This is an intergenerational problem, where the young must subsidize the high cost of elder care. If they refuse to buy insurance, they will pay a penalty regardless of how much they make.

The ACA mandated a thirty-hour workweek, setting a threshold for employer-paid health care benefits. The ruling affected companies with more than fifty employees, but the law of unintended consequences kicked in. Employers simply hired workers part time, working twenty-nine (29) hours a week. This drastically reduced the prospects for young adults. Part-time jobs and twenty-nine hours of pay are insufficient to meet minimum income requirements.

A Democratic congress, without a single Republican vote, attached an Education reform act to the ACA, redistributing nearly $7 billion dollars per annum from student grants to underwrite Obamacare. This rider led to the college funding methodology directly contributing to high student debt. If the government gives new college students a free pass, it means taxing the already indebted Millennials to pay for another person's education.

Young adults must subsidize Social Security without any guarantee it will be available for them. Regardless, elected officials from both parties avoid resolving this third rail of politics.

The political lesson learned is - the bureaucracy exists to perpetuate itself, regardless of the party. We need to vote for politicians that support the constitution, the rule of law, and present solutions for real problems. Policy is more important than emotion. Young adults must not drop out of the political process, but apply their considerable intelligence to discern the intention of the candidates and the consequences of their policies.

Academic

The second mistake was buying into the myth that a college degree is required to be successful in today's economy. To meet this expectation, many young adults incurred hardships and high student debt earning their degrees. Graduating with great expectations, young adults find those degrees mismatched to the needs of the marketplace. Forced to work outside of their field of study, they must take less challenging or entry-level positions to survive. Because high-paying jobs continue to migrate from America, the future remains bleak.

The mismatch of education to opportunity has another side. Jobs in high technology requiring college education beyond high school, but not necessarily bachelor degrees, are unfulfilled. Edward Gordon, PhD, estimates that current vacancy for high-tech jobs is greater than 6 million and by 2020, will explode to 20 million.

This mismatch has been worsening for more than ten years, yet continues for several reasons. The first is education economics. Universities will fight to protect their revenue streams, while the situation calls for an enormous transfer of revenue to the technical institutions. The second is the perception that tech school graduates are lower tier. Young adults understand this built in inequality, but participate by continuing to attend four-year colleges instead of technical schools.

A technical school degree or tech training is only the entry level to applied technologies. For example, a machine operator controlling robots can work up the ladder in educational step functions, to programmer, then engineer, and eventually into managerial positions.

The journey to success is not just where your career starts, but where additional education and hard work allow you to finish.

The third misconception is the perception that our factory system is dirty and demeaning. The following photo-essays are on our website, putting both the factory system and future jobs in perspective.

http://competitiveamerica.us/publications/Advanced_Agriculture.pdf
http://competitiveamerica.us/publications/Jobs_production.pdf
http://competitiveamerica.us/publications/Marten_mfg.pdf
http://competitiveamerica.us/publications/Waste_mgmt.pdf

An oxymoron - different but the same

The young adults and I are profoundly different because of upbringing. Many of us share growing up in dysfunctional families, for various reasons, but here we diverge substantially. I had a great deal of freedom to roam the woods, working with friends building interesting stuff from recovered materials, with very little direction from parents. We were free - perhaps too much so, but learned independence and self-reliance by failing, getting up and trying again. Entrepreneurship was part of our legacy. Our generation learned to adjust to a reality dictating four or five career changes.

Many of the young adults were stifled, brought up by helicopter parents in highly regimented environments, and missed the opportunity to explore and find out just how great they are. For these reasons, they are more risk averse. Young adults, however, must adjust to a high-velocity world of change, dictating multi-career changes, and **each must acquire entrepreneurial skills**.

Society must cease the meaningless discussion about helping youth trapped in marginalized circumstances, and take positive actions. In an increasingly complex world, there is a danger even more will be lost.

Technology training must be available, near to them, and affordable. Industry, given the incentive, can do more than government or education, and potentially offer these students an opportunity for positive futures. The price is the same for everyone, good decisions, hard work, and positive actions.

The young adults share my love for technology. I was fortunate, getting involved with computer science when it was still in formation, and developed the accumulated experiences into a successful systems consulting company.

Young adults are digital natives and how they use technology may determine the fate for large populations of humans. I also rebelled against the concept of humans as mere gears in the industrial machine, and that attitude continues. All systems must respect humans.

I support applied technologies including robotics, artificial intelligence, and factory automation. It will take applied human intelligence for these systems to function. An automated world potentially creates worse conditions for the young adults, but if this iteration of the industrial revolution happens in America, it will provide abundant opportunities of every type.

Those individuals who make good decisions about lifestyle, education, and careers will succeed in any environment.

Part Three - Values

8. Celebrate Our Freedoms

In 1776, the founders of our country had the courage to stand up to a repressive English government and say, "that's enough". They signed the Declaration of Independence, triggering the American Revolutionary War, our first war for FREEDOM.

Fourth of July in Las Vegas - Photograph by Wayne L Staley

The Declaration of Independence

IN CONGRESS, July 4, 1776.

The unanimous Declaration of the thirteen united States of America.
When in the Course of human events, it becomes necessary for one people to dissolve the political bands which have connected them with another, and to assume among the powers of the earth, the separate and equal station to which the Laws of Nature and of Nature's God entitle them, a decent respect to the opinions of mankind requires that they should declare the causes which impel them to the separation.

We hold these truths to be self-evident, that all men are created equal, that they are endowed by their Creator with certain unalienable Rights, that among these are Life, Liberty and the pursuit of Happiness.--That to secure these rights, Governments are instituted among Men, deriving their just powers from the consent of the governed, --That whenever any Form of Government becomes destructive of these ends, it is the Right of the People to alter or to abolish it, and to institute new Government, laying its foundation on such principles and organizing its powers in such form, as to them shall seem most likely to effect their Safety and Happiness. Prudence, indeed, will dictate that Governments long established should not be changed for light and transient causes; and accordingly all experience hath shewn, that mankind are more disposed to suffer, while evils are sufferable, than to right themselves by abolishing the forms to which they are accustomed. But when a long train of abuses and usurpations, pursuing invariably the same Object evinces a design to reduce them under absolute Despotism, it is their right, it is their duty, to throw off such Government, and to provide new Guards for their future security.--Such has been the patient sufferance of these Colonies; and such is now the necessity which constrains them to alter their former Systems of Government. The history of the present King of Great Britain is a history of repeated injuries and usurpations, all having in direct object the establishment of an absolute Tyranny over these States. To prove this, let Facts be submitted to a candid world.

While the Declaration of Independence served as the basis for our freedoms, the Constitution of the United States lays out the legal framework for governance and the rule of law. Following is the preamble.

Preamble to the Constitution

We the People of the United States, in Order to form a more perfect Union, establish Justice, insure domestic Tranquility, provide for the common defence, promote the general Welfare, and secure the Blessings of Liberty to ourselves and our Posterity, do ordain and establish this Constitution for the United States of America.

The Bill of Rights

Following is a transcription of the first ten amendments to the Constitution in their original form. These amendments ratified December 15, 1791, form the "Bill of Rights."

Amendment I

Congress shall make no law respecting an establishment of religion, or prohibiting the free exercise thereof; or abridging the freedom of speech, or of the press; or the right of the people peaceably to assemble, and to petition the Government for a redress of grievances.

Amendment II

A well-regulated Militia, being necessary to the security of a free State, the right of the people to keep and bear Arms, shall not be infringed.

Amendment III

No Soldier shall, in time of peace be quartered in any house, without the consent of the Owner, nor in time of war, but in a manner to be prescribed by law.

Amendment IV

The right of the people to be secure in their persons, houses, papers, and effects, against unreasonable searches and seizures, shall not be violated, and no Warrants shall issue, but upon probable cause, supported by Oath or affirmation, and particularly describing the place to be searched, and the persons or things to be seized.

Amendment V

No person shall be held to answer for a capital, or otherwise infamous crime, unless on a presentment or indictment of a Grand Jury, except in cases arising in the land or naval forces, or in the Militia, when in actual service in time of War or public danger; nor shall any person be subject for the same offence to be twice put in jeopardy of life or limb; nor shall be compelled in any criminal case to be a witness against himself, nor be deprived of life, liberty, or property, without due process of law; nor shall private property be taken for public use, without just compensation.

Amendment VI

In all criminal prosecutions, the accused shall enjoy the right to a speedy and public trial, by an impartial jury of the State and district wherein the crime shall have been committed, which district shall have been previously ascertained by law, and to be informed of the nature and cause of the accusation; to be confronted with the witnesses against him; to have compulsory process for obtaining witnesses in his favor, and to have the Assistance of Counsel for his defence.

Amendment VII

In Suits at common law, where the value in controversy shall exceed twenty dollars, the right of trial by jury shall be preserved, and no fact tried by a jury, shall be otherwise re-examined in any Court of the United States, than according to the rules of the common law.

Amendment VIII

Excessive bail shall not be required, nor excessive fines imposed, nor cruel and unusual punishments inflicted.

Amendment IX

The enumeration in the Constitution, of certain rights, shall not be construed to deny or disparage others retained by the people.

Amendment X

The powers not delegated to the United States by the Constitution, nor prohibited by it to the States, are reserved to the States respectively, or to the people.

There are additional amendments, but these form the original core of the Bill of Rights.

Individual rights are the foundational premise for the United States of America, clearly spelled out in the Declaration of Independence and the Constitution. The Bill of Rights guarantees these freedoms to every citizen regardless of race, color, creed, or sex.

Although imperfect, these documents form a set of common values, and the debate over the meaning will continue, requiring functional and responsible legislative bodies and courts. Our elected officials are accountable for the enforcement of, and conforming to, the Constitution. The President, members of Congress and the Senate, take an oath promising to uphold the Constitution, and are not above the law. When officials use the mechanisms of law to promote themselves and/or ideals opposing the will of the people, it is the ultimate betrayal.

The people determine changes to the values for the country, by enacting laws and amending the Constitution. Our system, based on personal liberties, can change quickly. Freedoms disappear in a heartbeat, without a fight. While the system is imperfect, requiring perpetual vigilance, freedoms must not be sacrificed on the twin alters of political correctness and a misunderstanding of socialism.

Problems hidden behind language construe false images. Resolution requires squarely facing a problem, defining intelligent solutions, and taking positive actions. Sometimes non-action results in what should be obvious consequences. The message of America is often lost in rhetoric and nonsense.

Passing the baton

The generations that survived the great depression and fought the evils of Nazism and Communism, valued our freedoms and suffered to preserve and pass them along to us.

The responsibility now passes to the new generation of leaders and voters, who own the destiny of the American dream and what form it will take. Young people are well educated but have a different perspective on the issues. To make freedom-related decisions, they must overcome years of educational programming leading them to socialism or worse.

The important point is - YOU OWN YOUR FUTURE THROUGH YOUR DECISIONS AND ACTIONS.

9. Religious Freedoms

Religious Freedom

Religious freedom has been the core premise for our liberties since the pilgrims stepped on Plymouth Rock. The religious composition of the founding fathers included Episcopalian, Anglican, Congregationalist, Presbyterian, Quaker, Unitarian, Catholic, and Deist.

The current religious mix of the United States shows Christians 70.6, unaffiliated 22.8, Atheist and Agnostic 7.1%, Non-Christian 5.9. The most significant changes since 2013 are Christian, down 12.4%, unaffiliated up 6.8%, and Non-Christian, growing from less than 2% to 5.9%. (*Source: Pew Forum on Religion & Public Life / U.S. Religious Landscape Survey*).

The Constitutional freedoms making Americans the most successful people in history are the same ones driving our economic activity. When government has the power to control religion, it can control the people, production/distribution systems just as easily.

Some people foolishly want to make this a political, rather than as social issue. In fact, it lies at the foundation of who we are as people. A loss of freedom will affect every person currently and all future generations. We may become one people again, without a party affiliation, and without a choice.

A government pushing the boundaries to gain power has little concern for color, religion, and social class, other than how to manipulate groups to achieve their purpose. Citizens must remember that centralized authority is antithetical to freedom.

The Catalyst

President Barack Obama, under authority granted by his Affordable Care Act (ACA), ordered the Catholic Church to violate core church values. Catholic theology states that humans do not have the right to block conception, and that once conception occurs aborting the child is murder. The administration forced a confrontation by demanding that the Church and affiliates offer coverage for birth control and morning-after pills, which are abortifacients. Faced with a firestorm of dissent, the Obama administration backed off partially, exempting the Churches, but not the affiliates such as the hospitals and charities. Backing further away, Obama agreed to have the birth control and morning-after pills paid for by the insurance companies.

The Affordable Health Care Act radically affected every American. The reason the Obama administration focused on Health Care is obvious. If government has control over medical care, it increases control over the people. Women's health is a straw man to draw attention from the damage it will eventually cause to families. The administration delayed the final rules until the 2016 election is over. Starting in October 2017, people will discover how much it really costs and how it will change their lives.

In the final analysis, it appears the Obama administration would celebrate the disintegration of the Catholic Church and all religious organizations. Advocates of big government see religion as a threat, and in nearly every historical case, government has attempted to eliminate or mitigate power threats. The key exceptions are atheism, which is often an ally of elitism, and Islam, for some unstated reason protected and embraced.

Religious Rights

Americans enjoy religious rights like few other countries in the world. It is this right that makes us great. It is a joy to drive down a highway and see a cross, a minaret, or a country church with a steeple.

I listened to the emotional power of the Baptist music that buoyed

Rural Cross - Wisconsin-Wayne Staley

Martin Luther King and the black community, as they fought for equality. The music of the Protestant reformation inspires me, and Jewish music causes longing for moments lost in time. The Islamic call to prayer reminds that diversity enriches us all. Attending a Latino Mass at Our Lady of the Valley Church in California, with the rich music sung in Spanish, is a great joy. Religion helps us deal with death and sorrow; it comforts us when things go wrong. Religion lifts and enriches us as one people, under God, giving us moral purpose beyond ourselves.

Face the Facts

It is time to return to facts and reality, not the smoke and mirrors used by the Obama machine to cloud the issue.

These facts are hard. The Obama administration has opposed religion at every step, except for Islam; therefore, one must conclude that if Barack Obama has the opportunity, he will eliminate the core premise of America, religious freedom. This is the new REALITY!

If the persecution of the Catholic Church succeeds, personal freedoms will significantly erode, negatively affecting all faiths without exception. Every American has the right to worship without government interference. Citizens should not have to pray for their right to worship.

Twenty years in the future, no one will care about labels. Our children and grandchildren will be justified in asking, "Why? How could you have been so stupid, selling us into government-controlled serfdom?"

I once believed in the incredible judgment of the American people to change destiny. The 2012 election shook that belief to the core. The people made an emotional decision based on the false sense of reality they were programmed to accept, and were gullible enough to buy into. They failed to do their homework, but even today; many are unable to evaluate the consequences by using critical thinking.

The Rev. Jeremiah Wright made the comment, "The chickens will come home to roost." Although he referenced a different context, in President Obama's case, the true character of the man emerged.

A free America, filled with opportunities, will release the pent-up power of the entrepreneurs, lifting everyone. A large centralized government destroying the foundation of our Republic takes everyone down.

It is never too late when free people wake up, understand the threat, and take action. As documented throughout this book, we are on the path to dystopia. Without religious freedoms, there will not be a free, nor competitive America.

Court assault on the church

The Little Sisters of the Poor, a Catholic religious order servicing the poor and elderly, continues to be a target for the Obama administration in spite of a Supreme Court ruling.

Attempting to circumvent the Supreme Court, The Obama administration unsuccessfully rewrote the rules.

The battle over religious freedoms in America has moved through the courts, with an uncertain future. Throughout history, the citizens counted on the Supreme Court to support our freedoms, but like the rest of government, it has become timid and unpredictable.

Obama and Israel

America and Israel have enjoyed a strong relationship since its establishment in 1948 as an independent country. Nearly from the first-day President Obama took office, his outreach has been to the Islamic world, which he supports with words and actions, frequently at the detriment of our relationship with Israel.

10. Equality

The joy of being an American is in having the freedom to write anything. We sit behind our desks surrounded by comfortable objects. Facts to support our opinion are available via the Internet, and picked to support starting premises. Liberals and conservatives alike participate, often in stereotypical terms, in the dance of lies and misinformation, in the name of "intellectual honesty." Fired into cyberspace, these missives have little accountability and lack bias checking by peers.

Affinity Systems LLC is a consulting firm, and our model is research and publications. Our skills are manufacturing, computer systems, quality, and Lean Six Sigma. Our work applies systems and thinking tools to analyze complicated systems - structures of all types. Action starts by identifying root causes through a process separating symptoms from problems, distortions from reality, then defining solutions for the problems. Once implemented, solutions must meet or exceed our customers and our own standards. There is no place to hide. We live by the merits of our work. Our mantra is to find and understand the facts to arrive at the truth within the scope of functional reality.

Having grown up in southern Kansas in the 1950s, I have personal experiences with deep-rooted cultural prejudice. Oklahoma, five miles south, had "blacks" and "whites" rest room facilities and water fountains. There was an Indian school, where children ripped from their tribal parents, received programming to think like whites. My hometown had separate swimming pools and seating sections in the theatre. Our family was poor and lived in a racially mixed neighborhood. I have seen, felt and been guilty of prejudice. It is easy to blame poverty, but prejudice extends to wealth, status, religion, nationality, sex, and sexual orientation.

As an adult living in Milwaukee during the racial rioting, I witnessed prejudicial conditions where anger manifested itself in multiple, different ways. There were racial riots and protest marches on the streets. I learned how to deal with prejudice from a very intelligent friend, a system analyst working for IBM. We were on an elevator, with demonstrations taking place on the streets below. The message was "Never group people. You must understand situations one person at a time, then as individuals within groups."

My friend was female, black, and right.

Reducing the human value makes it easier to subjugate people, and prejudice is not limited to race or social status. When I was a child, many Americans held Jews in contempt. In Nazi Germany, Joseph Goebbels, master propagandist, turned on the social programming machine. One of his tools was stereotyping. When an individual or group of humans can be "put in their place" through lumping into extreme categories, they are more easily mentally, then physically enslaved. A programmed populace looks the other way, just as the Germans did during the Holocaust and whites did when blacks were enslaved. While both are prime examples, the Native Americans suffered brutally under a policy of governmental genocide, accentuated by General Sheridan, "The only good Indians I ever saw were dead." In the West, shanghaied Chinese immigrants were literally beasts of burden.

Recently, I received a justification for why conservatives are misguided. The writer quoted materials proving conservatives are less educated, ignore the lessons of science, and harbor greater prejudices against literally "everyone else." It painted the extremes in broad generalities to justify the "analysis." Joseph Goebbels would love the matrix. The word conservative is interchangeable with Christian, Muslim, Jew, and Black,

Red, liberal, rich, poor, men, women or any other group. Changing the metrics reflects the correct stereotype.

It is my sincerest hope that Americans get off this stereotyping kick of liberals and conservatives, or identifying Americans by race. We are all colors, all opinions, and all faiths. Collectively, we sparkle like gold. My mantra is freedom. Slavery equates to a lack of freedom. It means that someone or a group of persons is attempting to control what and how we think and act. Our government, in this context, is the major offender, and working hard to keep us from unifying. Discernible people recognize the difference between verbiage and reality. They park their computers and go find out what is happening. Even as we argue against traditional forms of slavery, our freedoms are in jeopardy. The following story illustrates the point.

Doing research on the Gulf oil spill for a project, we drove through Plaquemine Parish near New Orleans, LA, an area severely flooded by hurricane Katrina on August 28, 2005. The effects of the oil spill were not visible, but the remnants of Katrina were everywhere. Following is a series of photographs taken in the drive through.

Plaquemine Parish, LA-Wayne Staley

63

One brave elderly man summarized the conditions in the area. He sadly explained the damage to the school, and the subsequent shutdown. He did not know how far students traveled to attend a different one. As he walked away, anger boiled up, that this human, in his old age, was living under these conditions. Where were the children? Where were they going to school? Had the storm doomed them for life? Worse, were they condemned before the hurricane?

Plaquemine Parish, LA-Wayne Staley

Plaquemine Parish, LA-Wayne Staley

The photographs are from March 2011. Why were these areas not rebuilt along with the rich coastal homes? The answer is Plaquemine Parish is poor, black and has little political power or influence. In the meantime, our country spent billions rebuilding Iraq and wasted billions on failed renewable-energy policies. Does anyone think this pattern is unique to New Orleans? The question is not why a black president failed to rebuild because George Bush also did little.

The lesson is obvious. ***Power is color blind, and it is all about power.***

This is an American tragedy perpetrated by both parties.

The sobering part of the trip was not being able to find anyone willing to talk about the oil spill and its effects. The Federal government shut down the free press. Most of the residents we talked to were afraid to discuss the situation because the government and BP had not settled with the litigants and silence was part of the agreement. Fear is the glue for enslavement.

Americans, through the Constitution and Bill of Rights, are free and equal people. The Constitution prevents the government from enslaving the people, either physically or mentally. Our government conceptually works for us, not vice-versa. The difference is profound. Serving at the will of the government translates to lost freedoms.

I returned with this thought in mind, "This would be the one acceptable stereotype. Having the ability to walk among our fellow Americans, and find them tolerant and respectful of others. All are free, in mind, body, and spirit, to pursue happiness, prosperity, and self-fulfillment. All are equal, under God, the Stars and Stripes, and the law."

11. Trust

"You may fool all the people some of the time; you can even fool some of the people all the time; but you can't fool all of the people all of the time." Abraham Lincoln

Trust is the glue for civilized interaction and essential for sustaining all relationships, whether personal, business, or political. While an intangible, trust is one of the most powerful words in our vocabulary.

A society, at work, at home or as part of our religion, share values, including ethics, morals, and implied responsibilities for others. Obviously, religions and populations throughout the world have different value systems. In many cases, although flawed logic, people interpret shared values as being for the greater good. Actions violating these implied, generic standards result in distrust and soiled reputations. In some countries, the consequences are extremely severe.

Reputation is one measure of trust. If people are truthful, honest, and fair in their dealing, they have personal integrity, and enjoy favorable reputations even when others disagree with their politics or perspectives. People with good reputations find it easier to get things done and participate in commercial activities. The reason, people trust them to do the job and do it right. Logically, everyone fails at some point, and trust implies accountability and taking responsibility, thereby starting the process of rebuilding trust. Given a lack of contrition for failure in relationships, additional distrust replaces what might otherwise start a healing process.

Following are key elements of trust that intertwine and support each other. These are honesty, quality, and integrity, being there for each other and forgiveness when possible or requested. We are all measured on how well we walk the talk, and keep promises and commitments.

Not telling the truth, either by out-right lying or through deception, has consequences. Friedrich Nietzsche summed it up neatly, "I'm not upset that you lied to me, I'm upset that from now on I can't believe you."

Given that trust is the fabric of our society, how do American institutions measure up?

Financial Institutions

CHICAGO (February 7, 2014) Americans are fed up with the excessive compensation and lack of integrity of top corporate managers, according to the latest data from the Chicago Booth/Kellogg School Financial Trust Index. The overall index's collective measure of trust held steady at 24 percent. Chase Financial institutions

Government

Following are the results of the Harvard University's Institute of Politics, trust levels from Millennials. This slice of our population represents our future. The numbers among other demographics vary, but these serve our purpose. The 2016 results vary, but not enough to change the overall picture. For more information visit:

http://iop.harvard.edu/youth-poll/harvard-iop-spring-2016-poll

	2010	2014	Delta
Federal Gov	29%	20%	<09>
President	44%	32%	<12>
Congress	25%	14%	<11>
Supreme Court	45%	36%	<09>
Total	143	102	<41>
Average	35.75	25.5	<10.5>
Total average change			<28.7> % total
US Military	53%	47%	<06>
United Nations	40%	34%	<06>
Wall Street	11%	12%	01
The Media	17%	11%	<06>
NSA		24%	

The confidence, or trust, in our three governmental bodies has dropped by 28.7% in the last four years, trending downwards each year. Business fares no better, with the same approximate percentage approval as overall government. The most distressing number is that Millennials have greater trust in the United Nations than in America.

Given this data, what conclusions are drawn?

Much of the mistrust is caused by lies that become increasingly obvious to everyone. These include the ACA, Benghazi, IRS profiling, fast and furious, the VA, illegal email accounts, the Clinton Foundation, the Iran agreement, and the list goes on.

The damage done to democracy by this administration will affect America for centuries. What is not so obvious is the deliberate attempt by both parties to split the American people into ever smaller, easier to control fractions. Part of the reason is the loss of common values, and rampant mistrust. Even the media, once regarded as the fourth leg of our government, the protector of freedoms, enjoys only 11% trust among the Millennials.

The big question remains. **Why do we let the government and press, the least trusted people in the United States, tell us how to think, not only about each other, but to swallow propaganda about what a great job they are doing?**

The Obama administration, including Hillary Clinton, has clearly demonstrated a total lack of managerial skill. They refuse to take responsibility for their actions, with either, "I didn't know," "I wasn't responsible," "George did it," or "it has been broken for 50 years, as the Veterans Administration. If they do not know, and are not accountable, why do we, the people that hire them, not throw them out on their well-cushioned butts?

Business has become fair game for not investing stored up capital and creating more jobs. The answer is that everyone hoards or saves when facing uncertainty, in this case caused by unnecessary regulation and distrust. When the government acts without consequence, distrust levels rise accordingly. In our personal lives, faced with uncertainty, large unnecessary expenses are deferred as long as possible. That is smart money management. Only the government seems to be immune from spending sprees that jeopardize the economy.

The last and the most obvious observation are the implication that Americans lack a common value system. The United States once valued the rule of law, one that our government appears dedicated to repealing. I submit that this metrics indicates we all suffer the same frustrations and in general share the common values spelled out in the Declaration of Independence, the Constitution, and Bill of Rights.

Summary

Ultimately, the voters are responsible for the government, through actions at the ballot box. We vote politicians into office, and when they violate our trust, we must vote them out. While many Americans do not trust the process because it is tainted with big money or political chicanery, voting is one of two actions available. The other is getting involved in the process itself. We have the responsibility of performing due diligence, finding out the facts about the people and policies being voted on. Citizens reap the consequences for abdicating their responsibility to vote. Voting is one of those decision points where not taking action means defaulting into an answer potentially more unacceptable.

Our job is to roll up our sleeves, clean-up government, restore trust to our systems, and provide freedoms and opportunities to future generations.

12. Our Immigrant Roots

America is a nation of immigrants, slaves, and indigenous (native) people, the latter invaded by the others.

Prior to Columbus, the population of First Americans numbered in the millions. The old images of small-scattered tribes portrayed in cowboy and Indian movies provided a false perspective. In reality, there were multiple types of complex social structures, stretching from the Arctic to the tip of the South American continent.

Mesa Verde, CO - Photograph by Wayne L Staley

We often look at the communications methodologies used by different nations to determine levels of sophistication. Signs and symbols communicating complex ideas mix with mundane information sharing in the petroglyphs of the southwest. The amount of lost or destroyed artifacts and history, while unknown, is massive.

Petroglyph - Petrified Forest - Photo- Natalie Groshek Staley

Lacking iron metal smelting knowledge, Native Americans made highly sophisticated stone tools. Although less technologically advanced than the settlers, they were light-years ahead from an environmental perspective, living in harmony with nature.

Immigrants brought technology and disease with a devastating effect on native populations. The government used the principle of manifest destiny to take the Indian lands. They destroyed the buffalo (bison) herds, the staple food source for the plain's tribe. It was the American genocide.

The lessons are many.

- Nothing is static. Populations move around the world based on many factors, including opportunity.
- Some group always suffers while others reap rewards.
- Technological sophistication usually determines the winner.
- The strong will find a way to win.
- Greed, necessity, and ideology make people do terrible things but only ideology escapes the process of intellectual reasoning.
- Humans can always find "justification" for brutal actions, and most ideologies are guilty of extremism at some point.
- The repopulations of large areas around the world through immigration, by invasion or invitation, are historical constants.
- Immigration frequently results in the destruction of indigenous value systems. We see this pattern repeating in Europe, as large Muslim populations create countries within countries.

- It is important that everyone keeps the issues in historical perspective.

Immigration to America

Immigrants from across the globe came together in a great, vital, and innovative melting pot, building a rapidly expanding and dynamic America. The strength of America, forged in the heat and pressure of common need and shared adversities, resulted in a system that still serves as the guiding light for the world. That does not make us perfect. Injustices exist in every system devised by humans and fixing them is always a work in process.

Tracing the path of immigrants, we stood at the old railroad station in Liberty State Park, on the banks of the Hudson River, across from New York City.

New Jersey - Photo-Wayne Staley

To the south, the Statue of Liberty proudly held up the Torch of Freedom.

The old train station primarily represents the history of the white migration to America. There was silence, where footsteps of millions of immigrants once echoed.

A sign at the station shows some of the destinations where the new Americans traveled, facing promising, but uncertain destinies.

Slavery in America

While most of the migration from Europe was by choice, big parts of it were not. Slave ships carried most of the African population to America.

Slavery is one of the most despicable ways that any human can treat another.

> **Slavery**, bondage, servitude refers to involuntary subjection to another or others. www.dictionary.com

My definition of slavery is "The loss of personal freedoms, the right to make decisions about our lives, without overt or covert coercion." It happens whenever one group of people is able to devalue another for personal, political, economic, religious, or social reasons.

Slavery has been a significant component of human life throughout history. Slaves, not free people, built the Pyramids of Giza, picked the cotton in the South, and built the railroads to the West.

Photograph - Wayne L Staley

Slavery was/is frequently covert and the result of social stratification in various societies. In the 17th and 18th century, slavery was a huge and thriving worldwide industry. Africans sold each other, and Europeans did the same.

Normally when Americans think about slavery, the image is of Africans brutally uprooted, chained into ships, brought to the south and put to work on cotton plantations. This is stereotypical and utterly fails to summarize the magnitude of the issue.

In America, slavery had three prongs, each with different labels.

Black African slaves were dispersed across the America and worked at every type of labor, although the tobacco and cotton fields are legendary.

Catholic-Irish were treated as sub-humans by the English and sold into slavery in the United States. Some were labeled "indentured servants." All received treatment on par with the black slaves, although bought and sold at lesser value.

The slavers bred Black Africans and young Irish girls like cattle to produce super-slaves, a practice that lasted for several decades.

Each wave of immigrants to America, some by choice and others by force, the Irish, Polish, Italians, Spanish, Latinos, Eastern Europeans, Middle East, and Africans, all started at the bottom of the food chain,.

In the West, the Gold fields and building of the railroads attracted large populations of primarily Chinese Asians. While not owned directly, per the definition of slavery, they were pseudo-slaves, controlled through coercion.

Slavery, by many labels is still pervasive throughout "civilization."

Common threads

Regardless of origin, native, or immigrant, America is a country of extraordinary and diverse humans, the survivors of immigration, serfdom, slavery, genocide, poverty, and yes, riches, and privilege.

Amazingly, nearly all demographics have united in common cause and integrated into one people. We fight among ourselves, but our cultural diversity is a strong human alloy forged in the melting pot of adversity. We are a unique democratic and social experiment. What we share is a passion for freedom and equal treatment for all.

13. Islamic Terrorism

While at the old railroad station, we looked across the Hudson River to the New York skyline. Our hearts were heavy looking at the nothingness where the two World Trade Center buildings once stood.

Robert M. Byrne took this beautiful photograph of the New York skyline before the attack. Print permission given by the photographer.

After the attack - World Trade Center photo-shopped out of the image.

On 9/11/2001, Islamic extremists viciously attacked the United States. The terrorists hijacked three airliners. They crashed two airplanes into the twin towers of the World Trade Center, killing 2,996 people and injuring more than 6,000 others. One airplane dived into the Pentagon, killing 125. The third attack, United Airlines Flight 93, targeted the White House or the Capital Building. Brave passengers, knowing they were going to die, fought with the terrorists. The plane crashed into a Pennsylvania field, killing all 44 people aboard, but possibly avoiding the massive carnage if it had hit either of its intended targets.

It is difficult to reason with fanatics believing they represent the only religion, and devoid of respect for our freedoms and way of life. They choose to kill innocent people by using the excuse of religion.

Islamic fundamentalists come from countries without a bill of rights, where women are little more than property, and there are few freedoms. Why would we want to import this value system?

http://www.billionbibles.org/sharia/sharia-law.html

Freedom and opportunity

Citizens create a country by uniting around a common set of values. The American dream is about freedom and opportunity, reflected in the Constitution of the United States of America. We are a country premised on the rule of law, and try not to discriminate against anyone.

Other legal systems are based on different value systems. Sharia law (based on the Islamic religion), in its extreme form, is the objective of the terrorists who flew airplanes into the World Trade Centers. They would turn the world into a Caliphate. The Constitution would disappear along with the associated freedoms, including religion and women's rights. If people insist on Sharia Law, they should move to a country practicing it, not attempt to force it on us.

Europe made the mistake of trying to let opposing governmental philosophies occupy, essentially, the same physical space, and the results have been catastrophic. Given the known consequences, it would be extremely poor judgment on our part to allow a fractionalized minority of immigrants to change the essence of our country. Most immigrants sought greater opportunity by coming to a free America and assimilating into society. Those immigrants are welcome.

The problem is that some of the people who wish us harm hide among those who truly seek refuge. This is the classic case of one rotten apple spoils the whole barrel.

Immigration is subtly changing the value system and face of America. The casualty may well be the freedoms that Americans call "rights," but in many cultures, are non-existent. Few of us want to live within a society without rights, and American women would not accept second-class status.

Hillary Clinton, running for president on the platform of women's rights, took home more than $100 million dollars from Saudi Arabia, Kuwait, Qatar, Oman, and the United Arab Emirates (UAE). These are the most repressive countries in the world towards women. What future favors did they buy from her? What message should this give to the women voters she passionately courts?

The women's rights movement, initiated by Susan B. Anthony in the late 1800s, eventually merged with the fight for civil rights led by Martin Luther King, Jr. The result was the 1965 Voting Rights Act, standardizing requirements at the Federal level. Complete equality is still an unrealized goal, but Sharia law would end the liberties we know and practice.

14. The Children Immigrants

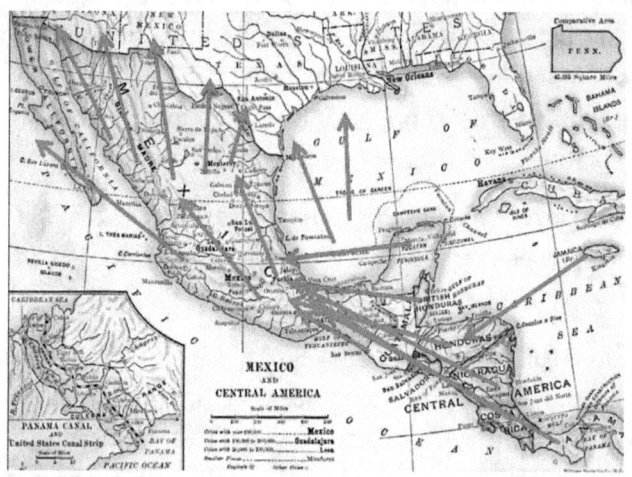

The Problem

For the last three years, tens of thousands of undocumented immigrants, many unaccompanied children, illegally surge over the US/Mexican border, and then surrender to the border patrol. The masses are multi-sourced, from the Caribbean, Central America, and other countries. The trip is perilous, made possible by organized criminals and corrupted officials, who welcome two additional revenue streams. These are extremely violent people, with little regard for life, who use and abuse the children. The criminals make money by funneling the immigrants through Mexico and across the border, but also by supplying the sex trade across the world with untraceable young women. Although the latter circumstance is undocumented, having some knowledge of the border, and recognizing that crime seizes every opportunity, be sure it occurs. Predators never let a tender prey escape. The immigrants provide a shield, distracting the border patrol, while criminals more easily smuggle drugs into the United States. There are reports that the physical and sexual abuse continues in the crowded refugee centers.

They come for many reasons, primarily opportunities for a new and better life in America, enabled and encouraged by conditions created by the Obama administration. The problem is not the children, who must be provided safety and with compassionate concern for their current and future welfare. We must find a way to provide them hope or at least options. These include return to their home countries, or finding families in America.

A secondary issue is health related. The immigrants are mostly untested for transmittable diseases, yet our government is distributing them across the country, setting the stage for potential epidemics.

Obviously, the opportunity is ripe for enemies, like ISIS, to infiltrate our borders, and the probability is very high they are doing exactly that.

Root Cause

The root cause of the fiasco is a commitment made by candidate Barack Obama to the Latino community in 2008. He promised them a comprehensive immigration bill to provide a pathway to citizenship.

The Latino vote was 67 percent for Obama. Without their vote, John McCain would have been the new president. In President Obama's first term, given both a Democratic Senate and Congress, comprehensive legislation was a near guarantee, but the president reneged on his promise.

Running for office a second time in 2012, faced with the potential loss of Latino voters and a recalcitrant Republican majority in the House, Obama issued a directive, not technically an executive order, through then-Secretary of Home Land Security, Janet Napolitano. Dated June 15,

2012, she issued the "Dream Act," providing a pathway for the children of immigrants born in America. Technically, it was a directive to ignore current laws in contrast to alternate legislation, but served the same purpose. In 2012, nine percent of all votes cast were from the Latino community, and 71 percent voted for Obama, assuring his re-election. Obviously, the strategy worked but it laid the foundation for the current crisis at the border.

Many of the immigrants believe they will automatically become citizens, with all the benefits accrued to that status, when they reach America.

Border Towns

Even given the fuzzy, illogical promise, I wondered how parents could send their children into harm's way, and then recalled my own experiences. Nothing has changed. Desperate people do what others may consider unreasonable.

It helps to have some understanding of border towns. Survival in resource-poor circumstances requires changing people's lives, priorities, and perspective, some for the better, others for the worse. To that purpose, here are two personal experiences.

At seventeen, in the military and undergoing surgical technician training at Fort Sam Houston Medical center in San Antonio, Texas, a group of us drove through the desert to Nuevo Laredo, Mexico, across the border from Laredo, Texas. We checked into our hotel and went to a restaurant, where young prostitutes immediately started hitting on us. Throughout the evening, as we bar hopped, this naive boy from southern Kansas was shocked at the open, ongoing parade of sex, alcohol, and drugs.

Years later, I was assigned to conduct the annual inventory audit at the Nogales, Mexico plant. I flew into Tucson, AZ on Saturday, rented a car, and drove to the assigned desert resort. Before leaving home, I promised my wife to attend Mass if possible. I drove to the border, parked on the American side and walked across the Rio Grande Bridge, into Nogales. There was an old Catholic Church in the square, and the sign stated that Mass started in roughly an hour. While it was early dusk, the Mariachi music signaled that downtown was open for action. After sitting for a while, a middle-aged man approached, and we spoke for a few minutes. Then he said, "My daughter, she is a virgin, and I can make her available to you." Married with four children, and more knowledgeable about human behavior, I simply said, "no thank you." The conversation over, he lit the candles on the altar, and when Mass began, he was the Acolyte.

The next day at the plant, I approached the topic with the Plant Manager, an American, and the accountant, a Mexican.

The plant manager replied, "When you have zero other assets, and you are hungry and probably have other mouths to feed, you sell thirty minutes of your daughter's time. Food, water, and a place to live carry greater value, and sex is an exchangeable, renewable, and marketable asset."

The accountant said, "You would be amazed at how many families send their girls to the border cities, to work as prostitutes. They save enough money and return home to get married. In many cases, girls are sold into the trade against their wills. It seems strange to you, a person with many available choices, but you do not have the right to judge people living in these circumstances. You can only try to understand how limited their options are."

I returned home better informed but feeling less human. I could not imagine in my wildest nightmare, with three daughters, how parents could do this. However, today, thousands send their children into the jaws of this horrible, monstrous system, where they may simply disappear forever.

The Desert

If the immigrants survive slavery and abuse, the next step is a hostile trip to the border across a scorching desert, by bus, packed in hot trucks, or by foot. Many will die, reclaimed by the coyotes, crows, and rodents. Their parents will never know where they are, or if they are deceased, only mourn their loss, knowing they may have contributed.

 In 2002, I drove to California, expecting to start a project, and while there, heard about people trying to cross the border. The project was delayed for several months so I decided to drive back to Wisconsin. As a photographer and analyst, and curious as usual, the decision was made to drive home via Mexico, a circuitous route, but more interesting than the interstate highway system. Against all advice, the selected route was to Douglas, AZ, entering Mexico, and driving east on Highway 2, to El Paso, TX via Ciudad Juarez, Mexico. (Google Maps shows the distance at 240 miles, and estimates slightly less than six hours to complete. It proved to be a very enlightening trip, lasting nearly nine hours).

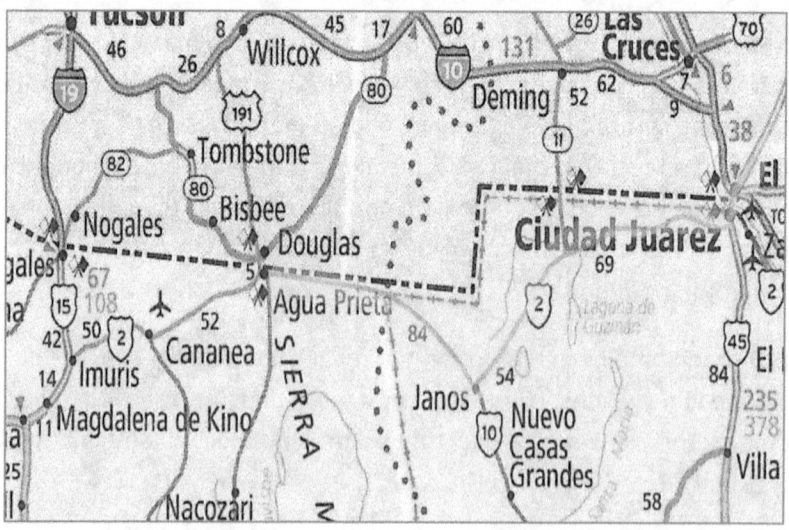

The entire trip, through the Sonoran desert, with the sun beating down, was very hot, and I ran the air-conditioning intermittently. Once, concerned about overheating in dangerous circumstances, I turned on the heater to cool the engine. The route was mostly dry scrub desert, but it was too dangerous to stop and photograph.

There were small areas with roughly constructed buildings, even cardboard shanties, and people of all ages walking around. About half way through the trip, with less distance from the road to the border, these shantytowns were quite large, stretching for miles. They were staging areas for destitute people with one objective, to cross the Rio Grande and enter the United States. Today, these shantytowns must be much more extensive.

Photograph -Wayne Staley

Driving past these shantytowns, with children, women and rough looking men watching, I felt very vulnerable, a huge resource-rich fish, traveling just a little too fast to harvest. Making matters worse, arriving in Juarez, the bridge crossing the border was closed, and I was soon lost on dirt back roads. Coming to a paved street, there were a number of brightly dressed people gathering. I asked three teen-agers, hoping they would know English, what was happening and how to get back to the bridge? They said it was Saturday night, when people dressed up and enjoyed the company of their neighbors. They provided directions back to the right route, and the safely of Texas, United States of America.

It would be unthinkable to try this trip today, across areas controlled by drug cartels, coyote's smuggling people, and Juarez is one of the murder capitals of the world.

The Hard Road to Perceived Opportunity

Returning to California later in the year, most of the associates in the plant were Latino. One, I'll call him Juan, was a tough looking guy who loves America, perhaps with greater intensity than most born here. His story was harrowing. He and his sister were from the Dominican Republic, where their father was a ranking member of the government. Juan and his sister were pro-freedom dissidents against that same government. One night, with an arrest warrant out for his children, Juan's father gave them airline tickets to Mexico. Juan was sixteen, and his sister only fourteen. They spent nearly two harrowing years, with Juan repeatedly and violently protecting his sister, before illegally entering the United States. They both received citizenship under President Reagan's amnesty program.

Responsibility

Regardless of how the Obama administration tries to spin the story, the President, and his executive pen created this cruel situation. He knew for two years it was in process, (from the time of the Dream Directive), but he did nothing to stop it, even enabling the situation. He hoped to shame the Republicans into passing comprehensive legislation. When the media started showing the children in make shift camps, President

Obama shut down the area and prevented coverage, ignoring the concept of a free press, a different but troubling topic. The administration even barred members of congress from the facilities. The entire situation is a brutal travesty of governance and responsibility.

The administration asked the legislative branch for 3.7 billion dollars to respond to a crisis they created, and got it. A Republican congress, complicit with the objectives of the bureaucracy, refused to execute the power over the purse. That brings the problem squarely home in other profound ways.

President Obama is spending greater amounts of money for the new arrivals, at the expense of millions of young Americans. The immigrants will have better prospects than citizens trapped in poor economic situations. *Where do American parents send their children to find opportunities*?

Of all the devious uncaring actions taken by this administration, none is quite as callous as this one, trading off the future of our children to achieve the political objective of keeping the Latino community in the Democratic Party. Coupled with the fiasco of failing on veteran's health care, the President exhibits little concern for life, unless the loss directly affects his poll numbers and/or legacy.

The entire situation has deeply diminished and blemished our great country. Tears of shame should cascade from every American eye, as we comprehend the corrupted situation surrounding the world's most valuable asset, the children.

2014

Megan Kelly, on Fox News, interviewed Jonathan Turley, a Washington University Law School professor.

"What I'm hearing certainly causes great concern that he (President Obama) will again violate the separation of powers. No president can take on the power of all three branches and that is what he seems to be doing. He certainly seems to be taking on legislative authority. He is not being particularly coy about this, you know he says 'this is what I wanted to get out of legislation and I'm going to do it on my own', and that does become a government of one.

It is a very sad moment but it is becoming a particularly dangerous moment if the president is going to go forward, particularly after this election to defy the will of Congress yet again. I can understand the frustration, these are two political parties that cannot get along but as you said, we have a Democratic process and a Congress that is coming in with the full voice of the American people behind them, that's what an election is, you may disagree with the outcome, but you have to respect the outcome. What the President is suggesting is tearing at the very fabric of the constitution. We have a separation of powers that gives us balance and that doesn't protect the branches. It's not there to protect the executive branch or the legislative branch, it's there to protect liberty. It's there to keep any branch from assuming so much control that they become a threat to liberty.

I always tell my friends on the Democratic side, we will rue the day when we helped create this uber presidency," he said. "What the Democrats are creating is something very very dangerous. They're creating a president who can go at it alone and to go at it alone is something that is a very danger that the framers sought to avoid in our constitution."

On February 26, 2014, Jonathan Turley testified before Congress. Following is an excerpt from his presentation. The full text is available at http://jonathanturley.files.wordpress.com/2014/02/turley-enforcement-testimony.pdf

I highly recommend anyone concerned about liberty, and the interpretation of the intent of the framers, to read the entirety of this extremely sobering presentation.

"Enforcing the President's Constitutional Duty to Faithfully Execute the Laws"

> "I recently testified before this Committee on the history and function of the separation of powers in our system. I also discussed how, in my view, President Obama has repeatedly violated this doctrine in the circumvention of Congress in areas ranging from health care to immigration law to environmental law. I will not repeat that discussion here because this hearing is not about the existence of such violations but the possible corrective measures that can be taken in light of those violations.
>
> Given the issues at stake in this debate, it is vital that we speak plainly about the current conflicts between the Executive Branch and the Legislative Branch. We are in the midst of a constitutional crisis with sweeping implications for our system of government. There has been a massive gravitational shift of authority to the Executive Branch that threatens the stability and functionality of our tripartite system. To be sure, this shift did not begin with President Obama. However, it has accelerated at an alarming rate under this Administration.
>
> These changes are occurring in a political environment with seemingly little oxygen for dialogue, let alone compromise.

Indeed, the current anaerobic conditions are breaking down the muscle of the constitutional system that protects us all. Of even greater concern is the fact that the other two branches appear passive, if not inert, as the Executive Branch has assumed such power.

As someone who voted for President Obama and agrees with many of his policies, it is often hard to separate the ends from the means of presidential action. Indeed, despite decades of thinking and writing about the separation of powers, I have had momentary lapses where I privately rejoiced in seeing actions on goals that I share, even though they were done in the circumvention of Congress. For example, when President Obama unilaterally acted on greenhouse gas pollutants, I was initially relieved. I agree entirely with the priority that he has given this issue. However, it takes an act of willful blindness to ignore that the greenhouse regulations were implemented only after Congress rejected such measures and that a new sweeping regulatory scheme is now being promulgated solely upon the authority of the President.

We are often so committed to a course of action that we conveniently dismiss the means as a minor issue in light of the goals of the Administration. Many have embraced the notion that all is fair in love and politics. However, as I have said too many times before Congress, in our system it is often more important how we do something than what we do. Priorities and policies (and presidents) change. What cannot change is the system upon which we all depend for our rights and representation."

Jonathon Turley is a tower in the legal profession and one of the most brilliant legal thinkers of our time. He has the courage to speak up.

Attempting to add to his commentary would be equivalent of attempting to modify E=mc2.

Mr. Turley would make an excellent Supreme Court Justice. The primary qualification is not political party; it is adherence to the Constitution, the rule of law, and embracing liberty.

His website is Jonathanturley.org.

2016

The Supreme Court punted the issue back to the lower courts, and stopped all penalties until the issue is resolved. Given a tie, the lower-court ruling that stopped the administration from taking action will remain, in effect, through the balance of the Obama administration.

Both governmental parties fail to deal intelligently with this hard emotional issue, one requiring bipartisan solutions.

We will offer a few obvious points to start the debate. One - the 12 to 20 million or so illegal immigrants currently in this country will not be deported. It is impractical and illogical. Two – setting up a system where they pay a fine to get into line for citizenship makes no sense. Where will they get the money, and who will pay for the bureaucracy needed to collect it? Three – the real victims are the children born in the United States that face extradition to countries they know nothing about. Four – meet some of the people and hear their stories. It will tear your heart out and prevent the discussion from becoming "just another abstract debate."

Listen to your immigrant parents or grandparents. All of them are real humans, but they came here through a lengthy legal process. Last – we do not know the solution. Perhaps if America simply annexed Mexico, the issue would be resolved.

The other side to the argument is the rule of law. Condoning undocumented people to flow freely across the borders create significant legal, financial, health, and security issues. Most of the people that advocate open border policies are emotionally, but otherwise unaffected.

Fact - America needs the workers. Fact- the people need jobs. Why is this so hard? Guest-worker programs exist all over the world. Many of those here illegally would love to go home to families across the border instead of constantly worrying about what the authorities will do next.

At the same time, we need to be extremely careful to prevent illegal immigrants from taking jobs at the expense of American citizens.

Summary

Western civilization will evolve its value systems in response to demographic turnover. This will result from the low-birth-rates in the Western World, and high-birthrates in the Middle East, Mexico, Latin America, and other countries. The effect is already occurring in Europe, and progressive globalization means it will eventually happen here.

The America of 2030 will be significantly different than it currently is. There will be a white minority, with a much greater Muslim and Latino demographics.

The question is whether all of these people, who come here with different values systems, will assimilate into one nation. The most important question is - will the people be free?

15. Free People Speak Out

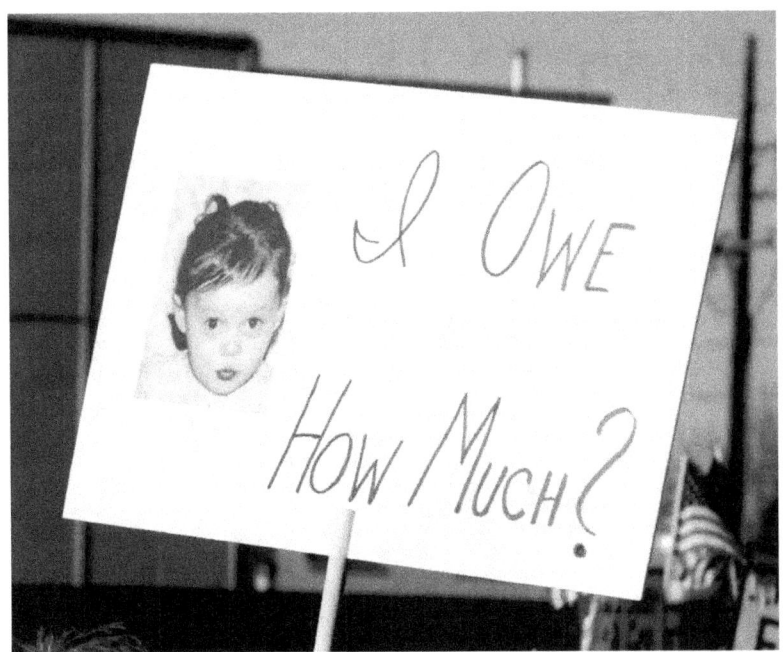

The Situation

Tea parties, tax protests, Black Life Matters– all are becoming common and all are directing their grievances and concerns at our government. Some groups, like Black Lives Matter, are taking positions against law enforcement, the very people needed to keep the people in high-crime safe.

By far the majority of the people living in disadvantaged areas, regardless of race, are good people that want the same things for their families as I want for mine. America, faced with racism on both sides, needs to knock it off and join together to fix the problems. If we build an opportunity driven America, there will be prosperity to go around. Look around; there is plenty of work to be done rebuilding the infrastructure of America, and rebuilding our factory systems.

Free speech is a time-honored part of the democratic process. The people must speak out. The government, however, can ignore or to demonize the effort. That means it is up to us, the people.

The Experiment

All protests have common cause at their core: the people responsible are not listening or are taking actions that are counter to the public's interests. Some protests are driven by the lack of access to jobs, unfulfilled promises, or inequality (real or perceived). In most cases, there is a breakdown of trust and respect.

Some years ago a business group I belonged to conducted a supervisory training session. All the participants were professional businesspersons. One of the exercises demonstrated how people react in a group environment based on the way they are treated. The participants counted out a number from one through eight. The session leader dismissed the ones, threes, and eights. In their absence, the remaining participants received the following instructions.

> "When the ones return, they are always correct regardless of what they say. Agree with them in every case.
>
> Listen to the number threes but regardless of correctness, disagree with them. They are wrong.
>
> Treat the number eights as non-persons. Move your chairs close together to keep them out of the group. Do not acknowledge their presence or listen to their input."

The number ones, some completely wrong but exonerated and supported by the group, soon relaxed, becoming open and vocal. All demonstrated secure positive body language.

The number threes, many of them correct, were increasingly vocal and agitated, raising their voices as they passionately pleaded their cause. Some finally gave up in frustration.

The number eights tried to rejoin the group but were shunned, their presence and input rejected. Before the session ended, in less than five minutes, some eights were angrily standing on their chairs screaming at their groups.

The balance of the group had the advantage of inclusion, and went along with every direction given by the instructor.

The Consequences

When the session ended, the instructor stated the ones, threes, and eights had reacted precisely as expected. They were not impressed. The negative feelings from even a short experience were very intense, and some of the number 3s and 8s were upset with team members for weeks. The number 8 in our group never missed an opportunity to remind us that we had "betrayed him."

Causes

Following are some of the conditions that set up protests. We see them in all aspects of our lives.

- When one side has fixated on a path of action and will sacrifice all to achieve their objective. Compromise is not an option.

- Where others have established the lines and parameters but one side does not agree with the rules.

- When rhetoric fails to match reality or pass the test of reasonableness.

- When one side takes an elitist attitude and ignores those with opposing views as "offering nothing constructive."

- When one side is condescending and rejects input from the other, labeling them obstructionists.

- When one or both sides lie or will say anything to achieve their goal.

These practices occur at all levels of society, in government, the workplace, in families and between friends.

Lesson Learned

Participation and involvement are keys to human interaction. There will always be disagreements, but when a legitimate and civil dialog prevails, there may be passion but not anger. If there is anger, it is temporary and non-violent.

Exclusion creates powerful emotions that may surge to the surface and even boil over. Eventually, ignoring the needs of individuals or groups may result in violence. The entire civil rights movement is an example of the failure to listen to the people and take positive actions.

Our systems in Conflict

Tea Party protests have disappeared although many people believe the current administration is attempting to reengineer our system from capitalistic to socialist. Depending on what set of facts a person accepts, this shift is real, wrongly perceived, or incorrect. The definition of socialism per Merriam-Webster is:

> Any of various economic and political theories advocating collective or governmental ownership and administration of the means of production and distribution of goods.

(a) System of society or group living in which there is no private property. (b) System or condition of society in which the means of production are owned and controlled by the state.

A stage of society in Marxist theory transitional between capitalism and communism and distinguished by unequal distribution of goods and pay according to work done.

One of the consequences of socialism is the redistribution of wealth. A certain amount of this occurs in any civilized society. Provisions are made for the poor, injured, unemployed, and elderly. It is unconscionable for the U.S.A., the wealthiest nation in the world, to have any citizen without healthcare, unless they choose to do without and are willing to accept responsibility for the cost of their care. Controls and regulations are established to help manage various systems. It is the extent, application, and control of these regulations that distinguishes capitalism from socialism.

It is the purpose behind the redistribution of assets and accumulated wealth that has some people upset. They believe our government wants to establish bureaucratic controls over every aspect of our lives. There is a concern that favoritism plays a significant role in who gets money, power, and opportunity. The Federal Government is layering expensive bureaucratic controls on all of our systems. These add cost, dilute the role of the legislative branch, and potentially reduce our freedoms and competitive capabilities.

While various reasons are given for the protests and different groups have come together, the core issue is control and power. The real fight is personal freedoms versus big government.

In a democracy, the people make the decisions through an electoral process. The assumption is the collective will of the people will move the country in the right direction. This system values the citizens as individuals who can manage their resources in their best interests. The people are responsible for their actions and accept the consequences of their decisions or non-decisions. The actions of the government are subordinate to the people.

The flip side of individualism is control by a government that presumes to know what is good for the citizens, and acts on that power through control mechanisms. The government has responsibly. The rights of individuals are subordinate to the government.

A pictorial review of the tax protest held in Wausau, Wisconsin on April 20, 2009 provides perspective.

This following photograph summarizes two critical points that Washington does not want to recognize, even today, in 2016.

1. Washington has labeled the protestors "right wing radicals" and has chosen to ignore them.

Truth: Republicans, Democrats, and Independents are angry and protesting. They feel the government is taking the country in the wrong direction, and today, in 2016, nothing has changed.

2. The promise of the Obama administration was change and transparency. Truth about the protestors:

Republicans - did not want the current administration and probably will not be happy with any of its legislation.

Democrats – Wanted a change from an insensitive and secretive government that lied and failed to control the economy. Those at the protest feel the new is a continuation of the old with a dangerous leaning towards bigger government.

Independents- voted for change but not social re-engineering. They wanted open, responsive, and honest government focusing on jobs, economy, and transparency. Uncontrolled spending and the czars are targets of their wrath.

The protestors were respectful of each other and, for the most part, they were protesting against government.

Protestors were law abiding Americans who want their country to remain the best and freest place on the face of the earth.

Were there extremists from both sides? Yes, because they also are citizens. However, neither group interrupted the rally.

The anger is not only directed towards the federal government.

Tea Party - Photo - Wayne Staley

Young people

Every generation has had a better standard of living than the previous one, a progression no longer be true. Government is at its best when enabling its citizens to succeed by creating jobs and wealth instead of imposing artificial controls and barriers.

Photograph-Wayne L Staley

Protestors were our next-door neighbors.

The politicians attended.

Some gave speeches while others observed. Some were obvious by their absence. All were respectful of Tea Party attendees and the attendees quietly interacted with the politicians.

In a free society, the people own the government instead of the government owning the people.

Free people must first speak out with civility. If not heard, they are justified in raising their voices with ever-increasing intensity until the politicians listen and execute the will of the people. This is one pathway to preserving our freedoms.

In fact, five years later, only the politicians have won. Both parties broke all other promises.

As the election of 2016 unfolds, the people are speaking out at the ballet box instead of on a picket line. The Democrats voted for Bernie Sanders, and the Republicans for Donald Trump. The reason is the same, a deep dissatisfaction with the status quo in Washington. The new battleground is socialism vs. capitalism, or big government against individual choices.

The old Democratic and Republican parties may collapse as the people put their needs and those of America ahead of party affiliation.

16. *Choice and Responsibility*

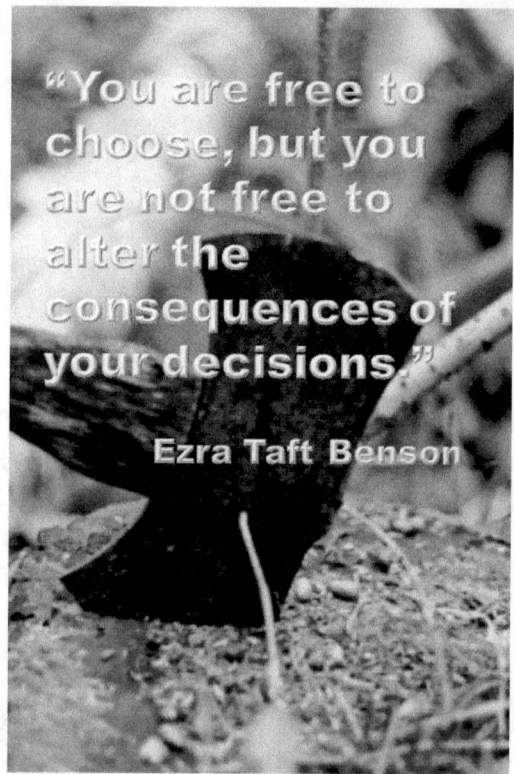

"You are free to choose, but you are not free to alter the consequences of your decisions."

Ezra Taft Benson

Photograph -Wayne Staley

Last Sunday, the homily in Church was about choice and responsibility. The essence was that we are all responsible for society and the choices made for the common good. The homily dealt with the need to take responsibility for the immigrants from Syria, South America, and Mexico.

Having just published a book titled "Decision-making in a Disruptive Reordering," the sermon raised some troubling issues about choices and responsibility.

Values

The core values for America are based on freedom (liberty) for all, individual rights, equality, self-government, diversity, and unity. Other values derive from the Old and New Testaments such as honesty, trust, integrity, responsibility, humility, frugality, and love of God. The obligation to each other, and belief that all are equal in God's eyes, are foundational.

Our increasingly secular society reinterprets choice to be obligation, and converts the concept of privilege and opportunity to "rights."

We cover the term "for the common (greater) good" in the chapter titled "Trust." For purposes of perspective, however, the core issue is who decides the meaning of "for the greater good" and what is our obligation to support these arbitrary objectives?

Political correctness

Political correctness is a state imposed on us by others, who want to control what we do, say, and feel. The expectation is that our decisions and actions will factor in this false narrative, and that individuals are responsible for any violation. Political correctness uses forced actions to legislate civility. It confuses freedom for individuals with personal improprieties. When forced to conform to artificial standards, we become slaves to the will of the perpetrators. When people act and think the same way, it kills the diversity of ideas and opportunities, precisely the opposite effect of the one needed for a free society.

Political correctness would have universal application if it had value. If a certain word or phrase is politically incorrect for one demographic, the rule should have equal application for all. It currently does not. I would immediately be branded as raciest by using words contained in RAP music, yet words directed towards other races are tolerated as "comedy, music, or art." While some may protest this double standard, it is free speech, and protected.

Proponents of political correctness value control more than the freedoms guaranteed by the Constitution of the United States. The promotion of political correctness could not survive without these freedoms. The dystopian culture promoted by political correctness would not allow political correctness itself.

Free speech is the right of free people, and as a vet, I think it is worth fighting to preserve our liberties. There are consequences for deciding to use hurtful language. Users should be accountable to each other, not the government, for poor social choices. Perhaps the biggest issue with political correctness is that political parties scream for civility, while bashing those who oppose them, then proposing limits on what the other party says.

It may sound contradictory, but when legitimate grievances are ignored, there must be a provision for public discourse. The Civil Rights movement was certainly justified and its cause, equality, was a demand to apply the provisions of the Constitution to every citizen. Other situations, such as "safe space" and the "campus reform" are the product of spoiled children. Universities exist to provide higher education, and to function as catalysts for ideas and positive change in society. That means maximizing diversity and the exchange of ideas, not shutting off dialogue. In a time when education becomes exponentially important, it demonstrates poor judgment to waste the opportunity.

Political correctness will potentially create an oxymoron, weakening the university system by shifting dollars towards a greater need. Public dollars spent on spoiled children, redirected towards the tech schools, could potentially offer greater opportunities to demographics trapped in poor circumstances. The workplace is looking for somewhere between eight and twelve million workers. Most will be graduates from tech schools with advanced science, technology, engineering, and mathematics (STEM) training.

People get their initial training for political correctness in kindergarten, where it belongs. We are not bound to make decisions on the arbitrary standards of others when the Constitution provides the free speech standard, and the Bible provides the blueprint for civil behavior.

There are terms and actions that are demeaning and/or harmful to others. The reason people use them is to belittle or visit pain on another person or demographic. The following photograph communicates an important lesson.

Photo by: Wayne L Staley

Don't laugh at me, don't call me, names, don't get your pleasure from my pain. In God's eyes's we're all the same, someday we'll all have perfect wings. Don't laugh at me.

Steve Seskin and Allen Shamblin

Our politically correct society rewards victims and punishes success. Our government and press use every opportunity to fractionalize demographics, playing them off for economic or political gain.

Political correctness is a **product, a reflection of larger circumstances.**

In 2008 and 2012, the majority of the voters made a decision and elected President Obama, who in turn appointed Hillary Clinton as Secretary of State. This begs the question from the homily.

Do these voters share responsibility for the shortfall in the Affordable Health Care Act? Do they share responsibility for the use of improper and inadequate statistics to misrepresent the state of the economy, or the nineteen trillion dollar national debt? Are they responsible for the whitewash of Fast and Furious? Are they culpable for the further loss of jobs among young black people? All of these have occurred on Presidents Obama's watch. Of course, some remain oblivious to the facts, ignoring that problems exist, or blaming some artificial straw man.

The Iraq and Afghanistan war, and the economic meltdown, occurred on President Bush's watch. While he took responsibility, the legacy continues to drain us emotionally, politically, and economically.

Without the war in Iraq, there might not be an ISIS, but the results are unknowable. If we had not withdrawn so sharply from Iraq, ISIS would probably not have gained power.

An issue closer to the homily is the current massive migration of people across the Middle East and Latinos from many countries flooding the United States. President Obama did not enforce the immigration laws, enabling the exodus from Latin America. The question remains, are supporters of President Obama and his policies responsible for the mass migrations and for doing something to help these people? As responsible citizens and members of society, we must support and take action to help those unfairly victimized by circumstances or lack of opportunity. Policy makers, however, need to be accountable for poor decisions.

Addressing the core question, we are not responsible for the decisions and actions of others. We are responsible for our decisions and actions, regardless of reasons or circumstances, and accountable for the consequences.

My value system drives decision-making. I believe in God, family, and the American system. God created all people equally, by giving us life and humanity, but not equal opportunities. It is a society's job to create an environment enabling opportunities for motivated people to achieve their potential.

We have the right to offend others, but civil dialogue defines intelligence, and deliberately offending others displays ignorance. Applied intelligence leads to problem definition, solutions, and a search for the mutual accommodation and advancement of everyone. The greater good is then defined as the positive pursuit of implementable solutions to societal issues. For those who have forgotten, this is the essence of democracy.

17. Salute the troops

Photograph-Wayne Staley

ON FAME'S ETERNAL CAMPING-GROUND,
THEIR SILENT TENTS ARE SPREAD,
AND GLORY GUARDS WITH SOLEMN ROUND
THE BIVOUAC OF THE DEAD.

Photograph-Wayne Staley

God bless those who have served our nation. Let us be a grateful people and recognize their contribution to the greatness of America.

Affinity Systems LLC, Competitive America, and Phase Four Graphics present this dedication to all members of our military who have served America and preserved our freedoms and way of life. Our thanks mix with sorrow for those who gave their lives, and to the families who lost sons and daughters. We back the American way of life and the liberties it implies. God bless America is a heart-felt prayer for the past, present and future.

The state of our nation

A presidential election is now in process. We have a black president, and woman presidential candidate. America has come a long way.

Unfortunately, the media separated America into blue states and red ones. In fact, we are many facets, shining like diamonds, enriching America, but making change complicated.

We need to put this in perspective.

The candidates are vying for the right to run this country. Here is where the winner will live and work.

White House - Photograph-Wayne Staley

That is the reality. All of the citizens and military of America have paid for these trappings of luxury and power. We the people are racially mixed, factory workers, farmers, information technologists, doctors – every vocation and way of life. Most are worried about the economy; jobs, raising our families, and doing the things that make us human and real. We are a good people. We help the desperate and wounded throughout the world. These include victims from tsunami, Earthquakes, and disastrous floods that engulf our own beautiful cities. We are responsible. We work, pay our bills, and support our country. We deserve a government that works.

Our Military

Our military has supported America every step of the way. They have rescued victim's worldwide and waged war when called upon. Citizens without military experience tend to compartmentalize wars as good or bad. The Revolutionary War was a "good" war. It freed us from tyranny.

The Civil War preserved the union. WWII preserved a civilization. To the military, a good war addresses true threats with superior mission, strategies, and tactics. The military has the backing of the people, proper equipment, and positive force multipliers. The objective is clear and unambiguous – win.

Korea was the first war that we lost and where the military was constrained in achieving its mission. Vietnam became the valley of tears for many, including military, family, and friends. The politicians that were responsible slept in warm beds and depleted the Social Security program to avoid telling the public the cost of the war. Politicians huddled in war rooms and dictated military tactics to a far more knowledgeable military command. Civilians were unaffected other than financially and emotionally. They intellectually and abstractly debated the war while American blood stained the battlefield in a far off Asian country that most had never heard of. The enemy was a people far less concerned about the form of government than simple survival. The intellectual process somehow ignored the lessons of a defeated French Army returning from the battleground of Indo-China. Regardless of the name, the result was the same. It was a loss caused by lack of political will, not military capability.

War protesters created a new music. Pete Seeger wrote, "Where Have All the Flowers Gone," in protest of all wars. Following is a summary.

> Where have all the flowers gone?
> Long time passing
> Where have all the flowers gone?
> Girls have picked them every one
> Where have all the young girls gone?
> Taken husbands every one
> Where have all the young men gone?
> Gone for soldiers every one
> Where have all the soldiers gone?
> Gone to graveyards every one

Where have all the graveyards gone?
Covered with flowers every one
When will we ever learn?
When will we ever learn?

These lyrics should make us pause and reflect on the sadness of any war. We will convert the song from a protest to a call to prayer. No one hates war more than the warriors do. They know that war is an essential requirement to maintain freedom for our children, grandchildren, and us. They know that people, some innocent, will die, are wounded, or suffer mental scars. We need to care for our vets, and make sure the American way of life is worth the sacrifice. The military will fight the wars, but our government needs to do a better job of defining when to fight.

Desert Storm, the war ousting Iraq from Kuwait was swift and decisive. The wars in Afghanistan and Iraq were not, but the military was doing its job, winning in both countries.

Congress, locked in partisanship bickering for nearly two decades, condemned the lack of political progress by the Iraq government while failing to address the relevant American issues. The America political process intervened. President Obama's administration, including John Kerry and Hillary Clinton, withdrew the military, paving the way for the emergence of ISIS. This extremist Islamic group is dedicated to Jihad and establishing a new Caliphate, and dedicated to destroying all civilization that refuses to bow to Mohammed.

Having served three years in the Army, I know that veterans think differently from those deprived a military experience. There is an essential truth. While the warrior is in the service of their country and its ideals, each is fighting for the sister and brother next to them. There is little time for ideology when bullets are popping all around you. The blood flowing in the trenches is not black, white or yellow – it is all red and mixed and very real.

The Marine motto, Semper Fidelis (always faithful), is not some abstract concept when someone is trying to kill you.

Pick your governmental representatives as if they will be fighting next to you. Who do you want covering your back? Who will stay faithful? Our military deserves a Commander in Chief that understands the realities of military power.

Our dedication

We dedicate the following photographs in memory of those who have served our country in every war and humanitarian activity. We include all who have served, warriors who gave the ultimate, those who survived, and those who stood at ready.

Where have all the flowers gone?

Here is our bouquet - Cherry Blossoms from Washington, DC.

Blossoms from Washington DC - Photograph-Wayne Staley

Unto Graveyards, every one - Gettysburg National Cemetery

- Photographs-Wayne Staley

Blossoms, tears, and prayers for every grave

Gettysburg National Cemetery -Photograph-Wayne Staley

Specials Prayers for the MIA's of every war

The remains of our military personnel rest in marked and unmarked graves all over the world. Their families still living morn the lack of closure. This photograph of the grave of an unknown soldier from the Civil War represents those who lost their lives but lie unrecognized in jungles, forests and deserts, their contributions often forgotten.

Photograph-Wayne Staley

Remember those who have contributed so much, some their lives, to make it possible for us to live in a free America. We are proud of our service people. Reach out to them. Call, write, or e-mail. They deserve our love, support, respect, and recognition.

18. Do the Means Justify the End?

Defining what truth means is complicated, but relates absolutely to the essence of our personal relationships, social fabric, and our position in a competitive world. It is an integral part to our search for the answer to why.

Lies and deception are political tools. The end justifies the means.

Truth, honesty, and integrity are personal traits

Upon discovery, lying and/or deceiving potentially results in angry consequences, with reaction often proportionately more severe than the lie itself. The greatest casualty is a loss of trust and respect. There will be accountability in some form, perhaps severe. The best resolution is taking responsibility, admission, and accountability. Regaining trust requires investment in the relationship, and honest actions, not words. This presumes others are considered to be worthy of an apology, and continuing relationship.

Match this private reaction to the public tolerance of near pathological lying by our elected officials on both sides, even after the lie is irrefutable. President Lyndon Johnson lied about sending troops to Vietnam. President Nixon lied about the Watergate break-in and later resigned. The electorate held President George H. Bush accountable for raising taxes after he promised, "Read my lips: no new taxes." President Clinton lied when he said, "I did not have sex with that woman," and was impeached, but not convicted of perjury.

Accusations often have an impact similar to exposure. For example, many think that President George W. Bush lied about weapons of mass destruction in Iraq. History must sort out the facts, and if true, the lie was certainly significant.

Few lies reach the magnitude or frequency of President Obama's "If you like your health care plan, you can keep your health care plan, period." It was a deception constructed to sell the Affordable Care Act, a massive governmental takeover of health care, to legislators and the public. Future generations will judge the value gained/lost from reengineering one-sixth of the American economy through subterfuge.

The polls showed a substantial drop in President Obama's trustworthiness, yet he compounded the problem. In an interview with Bill O'Reilly on FOX news, he stated there is "not a smidgen of corruption," on the part of the IRS, even as evidence to the contrary continued to build. After poisoning the water, the Department of Justice proved its corruption by passing on prosecution. The rule of law in America is a demonstrated two-tier system.

Obviously, there is something missing in all of this besides the truth.

In May 2001, former CBS News anchor Dan Rather stated, when asked about President Clintons' honesty, "Well, because I think he is. I think at core he's an honest person. I know that you have a different view. I know that you consider it sort of astonishing anybody would say so, but

I think you can be an honest person and lie about any number of things."

In a CNN interview, Ed Uravic, author of "Lying Cheating Scum" said "Every president has not only lied at some time, but needs to lie to be effective,"

The core perspective is how we perceive truth and consequences.

Most of us live by deontological ethics, or judge the truth by the act/deed itself. The opposite viewpoint is consequentialism, where the end consequence determines the merits/truth of the deed/action. Stated a different way, consequentialism translates to "the end justifies the means."

One example of the latter paradigm is the Affordable Health Care Act (ACA).

In his sales pitch for the ACA, President Obama repeated a litany of promises.

> "If you like your health care you can keep your health care
> If you like your doctor, you can keep your doctor
> Obamacare won't add 'one dime to our deficits'
> Premiums will fall by as much as $2,500 per family."

The ACA passed in 2010 as the signature legislation of the Obama administration. It passed entirely along party lines using deceit, lies, and strong-arm tactics. To get the last needed vote from Sen. Bart Stupak and the Pro-life Senatorial vote, President Obama signed an Executive Order barring federal funding of abortion through the ACA

Several years later Mr. Stupak said,

> "I am perplexed and disappointed that, having negotiated the Executive Order with the President, not only does that HHS

mandate violate the Executive Order but it also violates statutory law . . . . I think it is illegal."

(Note: The ACA allows abortions, and the Executive order stands in direct contradiction).

Every one of the above promises proved to be falsehoods, some to sell the program, and others as deceit to keep 2012 voters from finding out the negative ramifications of the legislation. The troubling question is whether, in his mind, they are lies or just necessary deceit to achieve his vision.

Sold under the premises of "the means justifies the end" philosophy, the net result of the ACA will be unknown until well after President Obama is out of office. It raises a greater question; do the American people call this a truthful process deserving a reward?

Yet, President Obama did not act alone, and the authors of the bill were a combination of business and political people. Every Democratic Senator and Representative voted for the Bill without reading it, an astonishing display of arrogance and irresponsibility to the people empowering them. Obviously, by default or intent, they practiced the philosophy of "any means justifies the end," hoping the result would be positive, and that constituents would reward them with additional terms in office. In my opinion, voters need to oust politicians violating the public's trust.

Voters may be blind to the deceptions because they trusted Obama to seize the opportunity and achieve positive change. That luster has not entirely rubbed off. Others looked past the dishonesties of the politician to the man, apparently an honest husband and good father. By their votes, all accepted the "any means to an end" argument. The end game for this administration remains unclear, and the rules constantly change, by obvious intent and deception. The key analogy is an iceberg, where the tip represents known lies, but hidden beneath the waves floats a mass of negative consequences.

The "any means justifies the end" philosophy breaks down quickly at the personal level. Telling one's spouse "I'm having an affair for the good of the marriage" will fly for one nanosecond. Why then, do we allow our elected officials to lie without accountability? Often failing to perform due diligence, the result is what we deserve.

Citizens need to fight for a truthful, honest, and accountable government. When officials establish their own agenda and use deception to achieve it, they eventually lose the confidence of the people and become irrelevant. Without a democratic process, we are enslaved and our freedoms lost. Meanwhile, the country will drift without leadership, from one crisis to another, exerting little influence over world events.

America needs a rebirth of truth and honesty, restoring our integrity and providing a common purpose, to build a competitive America.

Continuum

Sometimes other people's words make a better point for us. After discussions on "for the greater good" and "trust," the following is a powerful reinforcement of our position.

> "According to video posted Friday (November 7, 2014) by American Commitment, a conservative group, Massachusetts Institute of Technology professor Jonathan Gruber delivered remarks in October 2013 during which he explained the "tortured way" Obamacare was written that enabled its passage.
> "This bill was written in a tortured way to make sure CBO did not score the mandate as taxes," detailed Gruber. "If [Congressional Budget Office] scored the mandate as taxes, the bill dies. Okay, so

it's written to do that. In terms of risk-rated subsidies, if you had a law which said that healthy people are going to pay in — you made explicit that healthy people pay in and sick people get money — it would not have passed."

"Lack of transparency is a huge political advantage," he continued. "And basically, call it the stupidity of the American voter, or whatever, but basically that was really, really critical to getting the thing to pass. And it's the second-best argument." http://redalertpolitics.com/2014/11/10/obamacare-architect-jonathan-gruber-law-passed-thanks-lack-transparency/#ZHpDjlUrwp8Jb8Fx.99

There were at least four videos of Jonathan Gruber, one of the primary architects of the Affordable Care Art, calling the citizens of America "stupid." He was deeply involved in writing the Massachusetts health care program implemented by then Governor Romney. The Obama administration, capitalizing on the expertise gained on that program hired Mr. Gruber to help develop the ACA.

The administration argues the subsidies apply to all the states, whether in the exchange or not.

> "What's important to remember politically about this is if you're a state and you don't set up an exchange, that means your citizens don't get their tax credits—but your citizens still pay the taxes that support this bill. So you're essentially saying [to] your citizens you're going to pay all the taxes to help all the other states in the country. I hope that that's a blatant enough political reality that states will get their act together and realize there are billions of dollars at stake here in setting up these exchanges. But, you know, once again the politics can get ugly around this.

http://reason.com/blog/2014/07/24/watch-obamacare-architect-jonathan-gruber

The press was aware of, but chose not to report on the video.

It will be hard to find a better example of the concept of the "means justifies the end," and how it can translate into "my way or the highway," than the Affordable Health Care Act. How can a victimized constituency trust a government that defrauds them, or a press complicit with the fraud? In a very predictable response, the White House, elected officials, and the press are in full recovery mode, all throwing Jonathan Gruber under the bus.

The controversy and associated costs of the ACA will worsen. President Obama shifted the truly expensive and contentious implementation items until he is out of office. For details see:
http://www.nejm.org/doi/full/10.1056/NEJMp1403294

When examining the health care issue with any degree of objectivity, there are unpleasant truths. Prior to the passage of the ACA, health care costs were spiraling out of control. Nearly 50 million Americans lacked adequate access to health care.

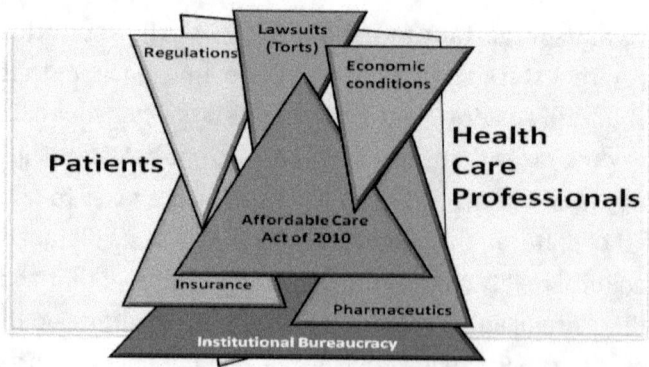

The above chart, from <u>Productivity Prescriptions for Health Care</u>, shows wedges driven between the patient and health care provider. Each

wedge adds cost and inefficiency to the process. The Affordable Care Act layered additional bureaucracy over the top of an already costly bureaucracy. A more effective approach would involve examining these wedges and shrinking each one down to a controllable size.

In the richest country on earth, every citizen should have access to affordable and comprehensive health care. Unless the system is converted back into a market-based system, and the wedges reduced, universal coverage is not achievable.

In a perverse way, Mr. Gruber's honesty was refreshing. He revealed the ACA as a hoax. It will not achieve the goal of providing affordable health care to every American citizen in spite of how much of our money the government spends.

President Obama is a disciple of Alinsky, sharing his method if not his value system. He taught workshops at the Developing Communities Project using his method.

> "The man of action views the issue of means and ends in pragmatic and strategic terms. He has no other problem; he thinks only of his actual resources and the possibilities of various choices of action. He asks of ends only whether they are achievable and worth the cost; of means, only whether they will work. To say that corrupt means corrupt the ends is to believe in the immaculate conception of ends and principles."

Obama worked with ACORN, another Alinsky creation. He obviously believes the means justify the end, and he wants to determine both the means and the end.

Part Four - Clear and Present Dangers

Experience hath shewn, that even under the best forms of government those entrusted with power have, in time, and by slow operations, perverted it into tyranny.

Thomas Jefferson

19. Alinsky's Rules for Radicals

Further exploring the topic of "the means justifying the end," one need only study Saul Alinsky's Rules for Radicals. President Obama and Hillary Clinton constantly practice the following rules of deception.

1. Power is not only what you have but what the enemy thinks you have.
2. Never go outside the experience of your people.
3. Wherever possible go outside the experience of the enemy. Here you want to cause confusion, fear, and retreat.
4. Make the enemy live up to their own book of rules.
5. Ridicule is man's most potent weapon.
6. A good tactic is one that your people enjoy.
7. A tactic that drags on too long becomes a drag.
8. Keep the pressure on.
9. The threat is usually more terrifying than the thing itself.
10. The major premise for tactics is the development of operations that will maintain a constant pressure upon the opposition.
11. If you push a negative hard and deep enough it will break through into its counter side.
12. The price of a successful attack is a constructive alternative.
13. Pick the target, freeze it, personalize it, and polarize it.

Source: http://townhall.com/columnists/johnhawkins/

Obvious by its absence are the rules Americans live by.

- Honesty
- Trustworthiness
- Integrity
- Transparency
- Responsibility
- Hard work
- Concern for others
- Allegiance to God and country
- Freedom of choice
- Freedom of religion
- Fiscal responsibility

Alinsky's Rules for Radicals are a recipe for social manipulation, and sharply contrast with traditional American values. Please note that rule four, "Make the enemy live up to their own book of rules," means to force us to practice our values, but not let us use their rules against them. In other words, take a knife to a gunfight.

While unable to predict the President's actions, as citizens we can extrapolate the future based on demonstrated performance.

We need to consider the consequences of a National database controlled by people in power motivated by Alinsky's Rules for Radicals, Ref Chapter 23-Information.

With this understanding, our perspective sharpens on the Presidents other priorities, specifically on immigration, Chapter 10, The Children Immigrants, an issue which failed to score above tenth place on any poll we researched, and the Iranian agreement Chapter 19 - Predator and Prey - An Analogy.

Why?

Another past master answers the question.

> "Hence that general is skilful in attack whose
> opponent does not know what to defend; and he is
> skilful in defense whose opponent does not know
> what to attack." Sun Tzu
>
> http://www.brainyquote.com/

Hillary Clinton is also an avid advocate of Alinsky, meeting him frequently, and holding seminars on his philosophy. Any student of her actions will find this to be an obvious and frightening point. Her entire career is filled with deception and parsing the truth.

How can society trust leaders operating on ethical principles that conflict with national values? This may be acceptable for a dictator, but not the president of a democracy.

 If the populace accepts or embraces these ethics and acts accordingly, they determine their own fates - to live without freedoms or equality. We live in a Republic and deserve the leaders we get by our actions in the political arena and the voting booth.

Our confidence in government reduces to one word - trust, and Hillary Clinton, an apostle of Alinsky, has mastered the philosophy as seen in all of her relationships and actions. As President of the United States, she and her husband would profit enormously at the expense of the American people. This is not a prediction; it is simply applying past demonstrated behavior to her future opportunity.

20. *Our Turn*

The 4th of July is a time to celebrate America, and the values it stands for, with flags flying, bands blaring out the National Anthem and fireworks exploding in the night sky.

Photographs-Wayne Staley

Sorrow

Joy is elusive this year. This week, I attended the funeral for a veteran from the Vietnam era. Following the Catholic burial service, he received military recognition. The honor guard was impeccable in pressed Navy whites, with properly worn chrome helmets. Every action was precise, salutes sharp, arms straight. The barks of the M1 Garand's in the 21-gun salute were as one. The bugle player for Taps was older, and the music wavered slightly, but still reminiscent of the nights in the barracks and field. The music sadly floated over this warrior, as it has millions of others, a final farewell to arms. The honor guard folded the flag carefully and correctly into a triangle, and then reverently presented the symbol to his widow.

The ceremony recognized this veteran for deeds, not words, serving America honorably to preserve our values and system, as men and women have done since the American Revolution.

The funeral was a reminder of how our military is under attack. The bomb blasts are political and unheard or ignored by the media. Further, there is complicity by the American people, who vote clueless people into office, often ignorant or uncaring about the responsibilities of the military. Combined, these paradigms are degrading the most powerful force ever assembled for freedom, both politically and economically, in the history of humankind. Following is a summarization of key issues affecting our military. For these reasons, although citizens first and military second, they are unable to stand up and fight for their rights.

For those not privileged to serve, there are a few fundamental concepts to understand.

The Chain of Command

The military is a tightly organized hierarchy, titled the chain of command. To preserve order and focus on the battlefield, it is essential that all military personnel precisely follow orders communicated through this chain. Obviously, without controlled actions, chaos would ensue with every battle lost. The concept is programmed into every recruit until it is totally accepted, or the individual is discharged. Disobedience is unacceptable.

The President of the United States of America is the Commander-In-Chief of the military per the Constitution of the United States. There is no requirement for a president to have experience with, or knowledge about how the military functions.

Article II Section 2 of the U.S. Constitution, the Commander in Chief clause, states that "[t]he President shall be Commander in Chief of the Army and Navy of the United States, and of the Militia of the several States, when called into the actual Service of the United States."

The oath taken by military officers is:

> I, _____, having been appointed an officer in the Army of the United States, as indicated above in the grade of _____ do solemnly swear (or affirm) that I will support and defend the Constitution of the United States against all enemies, foreign and domestic, that I will bear true faith and allegiance to the same; that I take this obligation freely, without any mental reservations or purpose of evasion; and that I will well and faithfully discharge the duties of the office upon which I am about to enter; So help me God."

The oath taken by military enlisted personnel is:

> I, (*NAME*), do solemnly swear (or affirm) that I will support and defend the Constitution of the United States against all enemies, foreign and domestic; that I will bear true faith and allegiance to the same; and that I will obey the orders of the President of the United States and the orders of the officers appointed over me, according to regulations and the Uniform Code of Military Justice. So help me God.

In the military, what the President wants, the president gets. He/she is god, and has the power to make or break anyone in the service, or working for the government after discharge. Following are some of the measures instituted by the Obama Administration.

Purging the Military

Embroiled in the controversies of Benghazi, Fast and Furious, and misuse of the IRS, the Obama administration moved strongly to remove all sources they felt were unreliable to their message. First, Gen. David Petraeus, caught up in scandal, resigned as head of the CIA. A year later, President Obama fired nine senior commanding officers. Speculation is that he feared a strong military and purged any potential opposition to strategy, policy, or actions.

Three of these men were involved, directly or peripherally, during the Benghazi attack, Gen. Ham, Major General Baker, and Rear Admiral Gaouette. The reports on their reactions to on-going events vary, whether they supported attempting armed intervention, believed that we had response capability, or if a response was even possible. In Gen Ham's case, reports go in both directions. Some reports state he was in the process of over-riding the stand-down order and was subsequently relieved. In his testimony, he indicated that poorly positioned assets prevented a reaction. Remember, however, the military serves the Commander In Chief.

Altogether, the administration purged hundreds of officers, for a variety of reasons, real or implied. It has become obvious that if a military person speaks out, the response will be fast and harsh. The mainstream media essentially ignored these unprecedented events.

The purging of the military by the administration stands in stark contrast to the non-response taken on civilian issues. These include Fast and Furious, Benghazi, and political activism by governmental agencies like the IRS. In addition, the corruption in the Veterans Hospital systems, while not ignored, was softly addressed when it was time to take names, kick ass and take care of the veterans. The President and media ignored or minimized every controversial issue.

Rules of Engagement

The Rules of Engagement for Afghanistan, reestablished by President Obama, put our military in far greater danger than necessary. Our military is not comprised of killers and mercenaries, and our government must not put troops in indefensible positions.

Allen West, US Army Lt Colonel (Ret) and former member of the House of Representatives, on February 13, 2014, tweeted about the Rules of Engagement.

> "As a former combat commander, I can tell you that fear is difficult to avoid on the battlefield. But on today's battlefields, a new fear haunts our troops; the fear of persecution by their own government. That fear leads to hesitation, and that leads to death."

No man left behind

On 9/11/2012, terrorists attacked the U.S. consulate in Benghazi, Libya. Our government did nothing, leaving four people, including an Ambassador, to die during a preventable attack, which took place on a predictable date, 9-11. All those involved violated the protocol demanding action, even if it fails, to save Americans under attack.

Ignoring all lessons learned President Obama exchanged five terrorist leaders for Sgt. Bergdahl, an alleged deserter, thereby making him a hero. While done in the name of "leaving no man behind," a political stunt that immediately backfired.

The irony is that politicians and press members chastise and condemn members of Bergdahl's unit, the same brothers in arms that tried to find and rescue him, some dying in the process.

The Veterans Administration

On this very day, our wounded comrades across the country are still fighting for medical care from our bloated, bureaucratic Veterans Administration. Every citizen in the United States, by virtue of having military protection, commits to providing them quality health care. Some of our military were on lists to receive medical care, and those lists later destroyed. Our government, of both parties, seems unwilling to mount the effort to search out each person with deferred treatment or appointments, and then break every speed record to provide medical attention. Of all the failures, the VA debacle is one of the most preventable and tragic. It is unconscionable that veterans die or suffer, while Congress dawdles and the President plays another round of golf, both protected by fabulous health care systems.

Simply appointing a new administrator did not get the job done.

The new head of the Veterans Administration, Secretary McDonald, filed no criminal charges, fired no one. It is another case of the bureaucracy giving an issue lip service, then once it was out of the news, reverting to past practices.

The Long List

This chapter touches the surface of issues affecting our military, but the ones covered make the point.

Our military is the protector from tyranny, the powerful force of men and women standing against dangers both domestic and foreign, which are hell-bent on reducing us to third world status, then slitting our throats. Recognized or not, our freedoms and military are under attack, and have been for nearly six years.

Our military is in a tough position, and nothing on the horizon appears to improve the situation. Certainly, no one wants a reason, like war, to improve conditions. The reality is, we are currently at war in Afghanistan, and radical Islam is at war with us, even if our government chooses to ignore it. We still live in a dangerous world and need an active and energized military to protect the homeland.

This is for my brothers and sisters in arms, all in lockstep though the march of time, from the Continental Army to present. We pay tribute to those still living who served in the World Wars, Korea, Vietnam, Desert Storm, Iraq, and Afghanistan and in between. Not all served on the firing line, but each made a difference, and none is diminished. All stood ready to fight for the equal rights and freedoms of all Americans, even those who would deny those very rights.

Say a prayer for all of our comrades, who are broken in body or mind. They paid a high price for our right to practice the religion of our choice, and criticize our leaders without fear of consequences. Pray for all of our brothers and sisters still in harm's way. All have paid the price in blood and treasure for the freedoms that make America the land of opportunity, a unique place where dreams can come true, no matter how humble our origins. Pray for the safety and well-being of all those who stand in defense of this great nation, still the world's greatest land of opportunity.

In the old Western movies, just as the enemy starts to win, the Cavalry rides in to save the day. Our job as citizens and veterans is to be the Cavalry for our active military, unable for many reasons to speak up and fight for themselves. It is our turn to defend them. Honor and duty bind us to that moral purpose. In retrospect, we failed.

The Military speaks out

Former Secretary of Defense Robert M. Gates challenged President Obama's commitment to the Afghan War in his book "Duty: Memoirs of a Secretary of War."

Former Secretary of Defense Leon Panetta published a new book, titled "Worthy Fights: A Memoir of Leadership in War and Peace."

> A book excerpt in Time Magazine recounts the internal battles over the timing of the withdrawal of U.S. troops from Iraq and whether a residual force would remain. Panetta and other Pentagon officials argued for keeping that force.

> "My fear, as I voiced to the President and others," Panetta writes, "was that if the country split apart or slid back into the violence that we'd seen in the years immediately following the U.S. invasion, it could become a new haven for terrorists to plot attacks against the U.S." He adds that his stance "reflected not just my views but also those of the military commanders in the region and the Joint Chiefs."

The military told the Obama administration precisely what would happen if America pulled all of our military assets out of Iraq. Following is an excerpt from Chicago Magazine.

> <u>Worthy Fights: A Memoir of Leadership in War and Peace</u> contains a surprisingly harsh assessment of President Obama, whom Panetta <u>describes</u> as having "lost his way," particularly on foreign policy. Panetta notes Obama's weak leadership, "reticence to engage his opponents," ignoring his own chemical-weapons "red line" in Syria, neglecting to arm the Syrian rebels, and failing to push hard enough for a residual force in Iraq. The result, writes Panetta, is the horror of ISIS. Panetta's memoir is so harsh in places that it makes <u>Bob Gates' memoir</u>, released earlier this year—Gates was Panetta's predecessor as secretary of defense—look somewhat milder in its takedown of Obama as Commander in Chief.www.chicagomag.com/Chicago-Magazine/Felsenthal-Files/October-2014/Leon-Panetta-Scorches-Obama-Praises-Rahm-in-New-Memoir/

These are historical critiques of a sitting president by past cabinet members. The good news is they are speaking out. The bad news nothing happened. We have a weak, disrespected Commander in Chief of the most powerful military in history. Compounding the problem, our country is slowly being drawn, Vietnam like, back into a combat role in the Middle East.

Taps

A Marine brother-in-arms has marched into God's arms. His fellow Marines gave him full accord, the haunting sound of taps, a folded flag for the widow, and a twenty-one gun salute. Dennis Groshek was a friend, brother-in-law, and a staunch American. He did not live long enough to see the rejection of President Obama's policies in the 2014 election, but he must be celebrating in Heaven. His beloved freedom-loving America still has a chance. We will all miss him.

Harvey Staley, a veteran of the Korean conflict, joined the ranks marching to God's eternal cadence.

What we can do

The President of the United States is the Commander in Chief of the military. The primary responsibility is protecting the territorial integrity of the union, while keeping the people safe.

Hillary Clinton has already demonstrated that she will choose political correctness over the lives of our military, and her failure to handle classified materials has put our national defense in jeopardy. Given the opportunity, she did not cover the people in the trenches. Her attitude on unrestricted immigration, ignoring all risks, proves she lacks the responsibility to protect the territorial integrity of the Union.

21. *The Rule of Law vs Chaos*

The Situation

The riots in Ferguson, MO, Baltimore, MD, and other American cities have ripped the scabs off deeply painful wounds festering for decades. The root causes are difficult to understand and correct and society has looked around for a scapegoat, someone easy to blame. Many well-meaning people, upset by the reports of police brutality, decided law enforcement is the "root of all evil." They have joined the chorus condemning all departments. The focus has been harsh, and all across America, our blue guardians have become a target for protestor's at all civic and governmental levels.

Since most of us live in more stable circumstances, it is useful to address the issue differently, and understand the frustration and causes precipitating negative actions.

Systems' thinking teaches that diagnosis and analysis must allow the trained mind to seek out the root cause and fix it. With the problem removed, the system will function effectively. If corrective action fails to fix the problem, then the diagnosis was incomplete or incorrect.

Based on this logic, America's problems are easy to solve by eliminating law enforcement altogether. Obviously, this would be silly and self-destructive. Chaos would rule and no one would be safe at home, or anywhere else for that matter. We saw the results of restrained police actions in Baltimore. Mobs destroyed property, burned cars, and injured police with thrown missiles.

The point is obvious; the actions of law-enforcement may worsen specific situations, but they are not the root cause, and broad condemnation is ignorance of the facts. The analysis must go deeper.

Frustration

Participation and involvement are keys to human interaction. While disagreements occur, anger is a temporary or non-violent reaction, but legitimate and civil dialog prevails. Exclusion, rejection, or frustration can dam up powerful emotions, potentially surging beneath the surface and boiling over. Ignoring the needs of individuals or groups may eventually result in violence. The civil rights movement is an example of failure to listen to grievances and take action to improve the various circumstances. The current situation is an echo of the unfulfilled implicit promises and frustration growing out of that era. Many of these are society's number eights.

Dealing with frustrations can take one of three basic paths.

1. Take out the frustration on ourselves with drugs or other self-destructive activities.

2. Lash out at those around you. This happens when the pressures build, and people lose hope. Violence, presumed to be a path to change the future and create opportunities, leads to a direct explosion of pent-up anger against real or perceived antagonists. This outlet leads to burning down or looting neighborhood businesses, destroying their own jobs and means of acquiring necessities.

3. Converted into a positive purpose, personal or social, if the situation has enough opportunities available.

Many inner-city residents lack opportunities. While most people know that social issues are barriers to individual advancement, crime rates are high, and the residents lack the political power to get real attention. While other demographics make political parties compete, often by providing opportunities, these communities are loyal to one political party and forfeit the competition for their votes. The government buys loyalties through aid programs, strengthening the dependence and removing incentives to take advantage of the opportunities that do exist.

In many ways, the black community have become voluntary slaves to the Democrats, who promise them much, but confident of their vote, consistently break those promises.

We have money for everything else, like governmental officials jetting all over the world, IRS parties, and the Secret service's orgies, all without accountability. At the same time, the police bust and jail a person buying illegal cigarettes on the street corner. This type of injustice sets a pattern. There are two sets of rules, one for the well connected, and another for the rest of us.

If we can find money to perpetuate and reward this bad behavior, why cannot we as a society find the money for complementary job training programs and address the real problems for social discord - the lack of opportunities and resources? The greater problem is for youth to break the dependency on government and take personal responsibility for their futures.

The problem is that we cannot help those who will not help themselves. The root cause is now apparent, and it is the dependence on government and inadequate academic attainment. In addition to demographic and social conditions, failure to develop and implement appropriate solutions allows the problem to fester. While blaming politicians for failing to address these problems, we voted them into office. The societal root problem is public apathy and dependence. Pogo was right. "We have met the enemy, and they are us."

Law Enforcement

Law enforcement is the guardian between social chaos and order. Teamed with emergency services, they protect our health and homes from crime, fires, and disasters. Both perform tasks that we cannot do for ourselves. For professionals in those fields, sometimes this means losing their lives or health.

The Black Lives Matter movement voiced some legitimate issues, but putting a target on law enforcement has had disastrous effects.

Do you think the world, with ISIS, the Middle East in flames, and our cities burning that society is safer today? Do you believe the police should stay home and allow the situation to revert to the old West, with people fending for themselves? If you do, look at the high murder rate in Chicago, and ask if your family should live with those same dangers.

The purpose of the police is to enforce the laws passed by the various governmental entities. It is not their job to determine which laws to enforce, be the crime selling illegal cigarettes on the street or homicide. Legislators need to repeal laws where the social consequences of enforcement are greater than the cost of the action on society. Our nanny state has created a plethora of restrictions, all requiring law enforcement. The use of violence and blaming the very people we hire to enforce our laws is not the pathway to positive change.

There will be mistakes, some real, others perceived, but the police must protect themselves if they are going to take care of us. When police break the law, they are criminals, but determine guilt through the justice system, not the media or for political purposes.

Here are a few questions to consider. What would have happened on Sept. 11, 2001, without emergency services? The emergency response to terrorist attacks claimed 694 police and firefighters. Did not the New

York Police Department establish a new standard for the entire country for preventing more terrorist attacks?

If someone kidnapped your child, would you call the police? What if there was no one to call? If someone came at you with a gun, would you yell for a protester or police officer? If involved in an accident, whom do you want at the scene? Why, given the social negativity towards the police, would they want to show up, and when they do, to enforce the law? Because they are professional, citizens, neighbors, and they care.

It is fair that every public entity requires an overview. Some police departments probably need change or transformation, but broadly applying that requirement to every police department in the country is absurd. If we are serious about law enforcement, put the Department of Justice under a microscope. They failed to investigate Fast and Furious, the IRS targeting program and numerous other politically sensitive issues. The Wall Street traders who caused the 2008 recession were never charged. This high-level abdication of responsibility is a genesis for frustration. When the press and politicians focus anger on the police, they hope we will forget who really caused the problem. We need to get real, because law enforcement is one group we all need on duty every day, every hour.

Putting law enforcement under the political gun has slowed the speed of response, and in emergencies, speed is life. It may be your life or the life of a loved one. The people comprising our law enforcement and emergency services deserve our respect, support, and prayers. To be there for us, we need to stand with them.

22. *Predator and Prey - An Analogy*

In early America, the majority of the people lived in rural environments, interacting daily with the natural world. When barbecuing a T-bone steak, cooks knew the meat source, and in fact, may have personally killed and slaughtered the animal. People rooted in the natural systems have always understood that life and death are inseparable, and that predators and prey come in many different forms. They also understand that life is precious, and when we kill something, it must be for a purpose, such as food, and not for the perverted joy of watching it die.

Some readers may believe that humans have advanced beyond these fundamental predator/prey relationships. For those looking for deeper insight, I suggest studying Darwin's, <u>On the Origins of Species - or the Preservation of Favored Races in the Struggle for Life.</u> Like it or not, science supports natural selection and the survival of the fittest. People hiding behind the concepts of appeasement (the prey can change the behavior of the predator), while preaching adherence to science suffer from intellectual schizophrenia.

The predator and prey relationship permeates every natural relationship. While some continue to deny it, humans are animals, separated by our big brains, fire and tool usage, and a presumed civilized structure. Some organizations, like ISIS, replace conventional concepts of civilization with a perverted ideology. Humans are in a constant war to acquire, hoard, and protect resources. To avoid becoming prey, and to protect our families, friends, and neighbors, people form governments and charge them with the primary purpose of providing protection from predatory nation/states, such as Iran.

In Urban populations, many citizens insulated from the reality that something must die for them to eat, fail to understand the predator/prey relationship. For them, the food chain is synonymous with the grocery store, butcher shop, and canned goods. Extending the thought, they fail to translate this stark reality into our international relationships, and the fact that some people, and some countries wish us great harm. The purpose of this analogy is reconnecting the harsh reality of predator and prey, specifically the recent agreement between the United States and Iran.

In 2009, Nat and I travelled the ALCAN Highway on the way to Alaska. In northern British Columbia, we saw a herd of bison several hundred yards to the West. We turned, and Nat, camera in hand, began taking photographs. For purposes of this analogy, they are the "Herd."

As we approached the herd, it became obvious there were different, concurrent events, and they unfolded in sequential panorama.

Photograph-Natalie Groshek Staley

Nat, like most mothers, focused on the cow patiently feeding her calf. Looking around, there were many other calves with the collective name of Future. Their mothers are Civilization.

Photograph-Natalie Groshek Staley

This calf appeared to be abandoned. Its name is Israel. Alone, it is prime prey for the bears.

Most of us are aware that few situations are precisely what we think they are. When we stopped the car, I took out a camera with a long lens and scoped around. There was a black bear behind the bison. This peaceful, pastoral scene was actuality a war zone between the bears and the bison.

Photograph-Natalie Staley

Photograph-Wayne Staley

This bear was not happy and heading straight towards us. I took this photo and ducked to safety. It disappeared in the brush, but two bears were now involved. We label this bear, Russia, because like that country, it is dark, massive, dangerous, and unpredictable.

Photograph-Wayne Staley

Natalie spotted another bear. This one was not fully-grown.

People sometimes question if wild animals can think. This bear ran up to the road, stood up, and looked both ways before running across. Because this little bear is cute, some people are attracted to it, while in fact, it gets more dangerous as it grows, just like ISIS.

We now have three bears around the herd.

Photographs-Natalie Groshek Staley

Following ISIS, a fourth bear (next page) shot across the road and up the hill. Its demeanor was very hostile. Of the bears we have photographed, this is the most fearsome. It defiantly overlooked the killing field, waiting for us to leave.

Photographs - Wayne L Staley

This is much like Iran, a mean spirited, hostile, and avowed enemy of the United States, Israel, and Western civilization. Iran is preparing the means to destroy its real and perceived enemies, and needs only the opportunity to strike. Anyone who thinks Iran is sincere needs to study international business. In some cultures, shrewdness is a greater virtue than honesty. Deals made with infidels are meaningless. For a reference closer to home, read Saul Alinsky's Rules for Radicals.

 While photographing Iran, a fifth bear crossed a dry, rocky, washed-out area. This bear was grunting and limping, its front leg severely damaged. The fact that five bears were near the herd was probably mutual opportunity not cooperation. Russia, ISIS, and Iran are (probably) not working in direct concert, and have conflicts between themselves, but share mutual opportunities to take advantage of the West.

Photograph-Wayne Staley

We continue the analogy by returning to the bison. Their status now changes to prey, but obviously not one easily taken down. Given the location, time, and circumstance, it is reasonable to assume the last bear sustained a massive blow from one of the bison. The herd has the capability to defend itself. One predator's death will not affect the actions of, nor deter, the others. There are casualties in every conflict.

First, we know that mothers, wildlife or human, will fight to the death to save their offspring. Additional useful facts are that bison are massive, and bulls weigh approximately 2000 pounds, cows around 1100, and newborn calves weigh about 45 pounds. A black bear is 150-300 pounds, although some may be double that weight.

The herd is analogous to the United States. We are larger and stronger than Iran, ISIS, and even Russia. We give away our power by trying to appease our enemies, just as Arthur Neville Chamberlain conceded to Adolf Hitler. Instead, we need to confront our enemies. Strength logically implies courage, but instead of positive actions, our leaders surrender our power to weaker adversaries, getting nothing in return.

Bison fight with each other for territory and breeding rights, easily

Photograph-Wayne Staley

equated to self-interest. Preoccupied with this selfish head banging, the remaining male is free to take independent action. I will label the two males fighting with each other Republicans and Democrats, and the one in the background, ignoring the others, Mr. President.

Our elected officials, of both parties, are more concerned about retaining office and growing personal power and wealth than protecting the people. We have three branches of government, and all lack the courage or will to protect the country and civilization from our enemies.

We could not take pictures of Mr. President cutting dangerous deals with Iran, but he did.

Our divided people, in many cases, ignore the fact that bears (our enemies) are predators and want to eat our young. Some members of our herd think they are cuddly teddy bears, instead of a clear and present danger. They believe that Iran, a country still chanting, "Death to America," will become less predatory if we pat them on the head, and feed them money. Imagine feeding the bears. Death would be brutal, and they would dine on more than the hand who fed them.

Leaving the bison, we traveled just a few miles until Nat photographed this bear. Larger than those hunting the bison, we will call it China.

Photograph-Natalie Groshek Staley

China, while not a visible player in the Iran deal, is certainly involved on many levels. China is a predator and a competitor, not a friend, economically preying on the United States with impunity. We need to face the facts. Our elected officials are scared to death of China, and hope all contentions will simply go away. This amounts to self-deception.

Photograph-Wayne Staley

This male bison was one of the largest and potentially most dangerous protectors on the field. He stood alone, waiting for a call to action. Our metaphor for this bull is Military, which allows the herd to defend itself. Instead of making Military stronger to protect the Herd, Mr. President continues to weaken its capability, in direct violation of his primary purpose for being President, protecting the homeland from predators.

The bison are smart, and know the enemy is coming. Failure to grasp that reality ourselves means we are not as smart. America has abandoned Israel, but unlike other potential prey, if Iran nukes Israel,

Iran will disappear in a nuclear cloud, putting the world on a path to annihilation.

If America is weak and subservient, Iran, ISIS, Russia, and China will feast on America's Future and destroy our Civilization. If we make non-enforceable deals, and/or fight among ourselves, we accommodate our enemies. If we emasculate our military, the predators will have a killing field in our pasture, devouring America's Future and Civilization.

Obama and Iran

President Obama signed an arm's agreement with Iran, a country vowing to replace the government in Israel. (There is a controversy over the interpretation for the phrase then Iranian President Mahmoud Ahmadinejad used, but the meaning is clear, the elimination of the nation of Israel as a democratic Jewish state). The agreement with Iran essentially removes the barriers to their development of weapons systems. At the end of the agreement, they are free to build nuclear weapons. To seal the deal, the United States released somewhere between $100 and $150 billion dollars held as sanctions for earlier agreement violations. Iran has already blown off the agreement, and is doing business with countries all over the world- e.g. purchasing weapons from Russia.

If Iran develops an atomic bomb, the world will instantly become a far more dangerous place, putting Israel and America in imminent danger.

Sometimes no deal is the best deal. We invited the enemy to a meal and left the guards outside the door. Our children and grandchildren are on the menu. A treaty directly threatening America is treason. Party politics took precedence over national security.

The Middle East

The Middle East is in turmoil. The United States entered a Faustian agreement with Iran; we turned our backs on Israel, and invited chaos in Libya by ousting Gaddafi. This led directly to the terrorist attack on the American compound at Benghazi.

President Obama ordered the military to do everything possible to save the people inside the embassy, but failed the basic management principle of follow-up to make sure his orders were obeyed. While the reason is buried, he did attend a campaign fundraiser the next day in Las Vegas, and skipped the Intelligence briefings. His election was more important the Americans in the Embassy.

Secretary of State Clinton held back the military response for hours, trying to decide which politically correct uniform was appropriate. Not only did she let the attack continue and kill four people, but also she committed insubordination by disobeying the president's order. While contemplating what attire the military needed, she conspired with associates on a lie, blaming the attack on a video instead of terrorists.

An interesting sidebar- although our government knows who many of the attackers are, they have done little to hold them accountable.

The big, dark secret

There is a huge political, secret iceberg buried under the opaque sea of our ignorance about reality in the Middle East, further concealed by the absence of government transparency.

Some of the facts are coming out. Hillary Clinton and the Clinton Foundation received massive amounts of money from the Persian Gulf states.

The Daily Caller reports:

> A Daily Caller News Foundation investigation reveals
> that Bill and Hillary Clinton received at least $100
> million from autocratic Persian Gulf states and
> their leaders, potentially undermining Democratic
> presidential candidate Hillary's claim she can carry out
> independent Middle East policies.
>
> As a presidential candidate, the amount of foreign cash
> the Clintons have amassed from the Persian Gulf states
> is "simply unprecedented," says national security
> analyst Patrick Poole.
>
> "These regimes are buying access. You've got the
> Saudis. You've got the Kuwaitis, Oman, Qatar and the
> UAE. There are massive conflicts of interest. It's beyond
> comprehension," Poole told The DCNF in an interview.

http://dailycaller.com/2016/05/11/exclusive-persian-gulf-sheikhs-gave-bill-hillary-100-million/#ixzz4FC7us5vC

I recommend readers visit this site, and others. Find out what commitments Mrs. Clinton has to people wishing us great harm. How would these relationships affect her actions as the President of the United States?

The Kuwaiti newspaper Al-Jarida reports that President Obama lusts for the job as Secretary-General of the United States. He has spent eight years redistributing American wealth across the globe, bowing to Muslim leaders, and making deals with enemies like Iran. We can only hope the purpose was not influence peddling to obtain the job "President of the World." If that happens, he would do everything to finish the job he started, to bring America to her knees, and destroy our liberties, starting with small arm's weapons confiscation.

Given the low esteem most of the world has for him, perhaps it will remain only a wish in Obama's mind.

23. The Bear is BACK!

Photograph by Natalie Groshek Staley

The trip to Alaska provided another analogy, this one addressing economic issues. Natalie took the images for this photo/essay under difficult conditions. Collectively, they tell a great and appropriate story.

A fisherman was standing on a rock in the middle of the Chilkoot River north west of Haines, Alaska. It was a productive day for him, with three large Sockeye salmon attached to his belt.

A brown bear walked up the road and into the river, slowly approaching the fisherman from behind. This bear was not interested in the fisherman, only his high-fat content salmon.

Natalie caught the moment in the next two photographs.

The man turned, saw the bear, and intelligently and quickly unhooked the stringer, watching his prize catch of fish wash downstream.

Please note the parallel situation depicted on the sign, down to the red jacket and the position of the bear.

A short distance upstream, a weir stretched across the river, functioning like a sieve, letting the water pass through while forcing the salmon to the center (marked with the red triangle), where they are counted. This concentrates fish, making them easy targets for the bear.

Ambling up the road to the wier, the bear repeatedly jumped in the water, caught fish, carried them to shore, ripped them to pieces, and ate them. While appearing to be greedy, the bear must store enough fat to sustain life while hibernating through a tough Alaskan winter.

Photograph by
Natalie Groshek Staley

Analogy

The financial bear periodically ravages the economy, and while America is not in an economic crisis, we are in a slow no-growth period. The bear is prowling, knowing that we if continue our current practices, as presented in the previous chapter, it will feast yet again on our savings and wealth.

While the pundits and talking heads differ about the reasons for the economic stagnation, be it China, the world economy or an overheated stock market, the answer is as obvious as the bear eating the fish. We have lost our sense of priority, survival instincts, and national purpose.

There are a number of reality shows on television such as "Naked and Afraid," and "Alone." In summary, individuals, pairs, or groups of people are taken to remote sites with scarce or difficult to acquire resources, such as water and food. The contestants, with a limited number of tools, must survive for varying periods. They can quit at any time, and the reward varies from little to significant.

The situation is primal, reducing humans to one level above other animals. Their priorities are safety, shelter, fire, water, and food. The order is dependent upon circumstances. Safety must be first, because an injury without medical care may result in death.

The tests are brutal but survival is situational, and the failure to maintain these five priorities in relation to specific conditions ends badly for the contestants.

The issue, for individuals and governments alike, is establishing the right priorities for our survival. This requires making choices about where to invest time and money. Situational assessments determine which dangers immediately affect our life, and deserve the highest priority. Once that is accomplished, we need the ability to sustain it and prepare for the future. In America, this includes taking on significant projects providing long-term benefits. Two examples of leaders able to transform society with big ideas and deeds were President Dwight D. Eisenhower, building the interstate highway system, and President John F. Kennedy, who championed the space program.

In 2008, the bears feasted on our economy. Following the collapse, Americans had the chance to achieve energy independence, build new factory systems, disengage in middle-eastern oil markets, afford a powerful military, and create sustainable food sources. We ignored opportunities to fund big science projects. We could have developed disruptive technological systems capable of sustaining human civilization far into the future. Sadly, even the space program, history's greatest science project and generator of technology, was truncated.

Instead of economic priorities, our government focused on social issues such as health care, immigration, regulations, redistribution, and racial parity, all components of control. While these are important issues, they prevented entrepreneurs from generating more jobs and creating better technological solutions. In the process, the national debt multiplied, making it difficult to negotiate with China, the biggest bear in the forest, and our largest creditor.

Right now, the United States, along with most of the world, is losing the game of survival. While still the world's strongest economy, we continue to downsize, redistribute our assets, and sacrifice opportunities for many demographics. We have all the tools to survive and provide abundance for every citizen, yet refuse to put these tools to work.

The full economic recovery, associated with every other recession, never occurred.

One problem is a lack of situational awareness and ordering priorities required to survive. The major reason, sadly, is the failure of leadership and lack of vision by both parties. For these reasons, the bears are back. Actually, they never went away, but waited to ambush a society operating with confused survival priorities.

We need to recreate a growth economy, one where the bull returns and drives away the bears bent on devouring our future. In other words, activate our survival priorities, and build a sustainable opportunity driven society for current and future generations of Americans.

I am optimistic. The massive science and technological projects needed to sustain humans and the environment are challenges to our leadership, intelligence, and capabilities. We are Americans, and can make it happen.

24. *Information*

Information is a tool for great good or evil, depending on how and who uses it. It is critical to understand that information is the new currency of global exchange. Governments, industry, and individuals spend billions of dollars in search of every type of information. Our personal data is our most valuable and highly sought-after possession, directly linking to our wealth and personal power. Every citizen of the United States, and most of the world, is in danger of losing personal freedoms by the misappropriation or misapplication of their invisible data self.

 As consultants, we are information management professionals and understand how close it resides to the power apex. The more actionable data one has, the greater the opportunity to create information and take advantage of people, turning situations to our cause or profit. Information is the competitive edge, enabling every type of physical action or reaction. This applies to all of society, personal relationships, health care, business competition, politics, and government. Please note the distinction between politics and government because later in this Newsletter, the difference is quite relevant.

There are cause and consequences of rapidly merging information databases, potentially into a National Database of You and Me. These data are useful to manipulate or coerce us into taking action against our free will, or for the greater good as defined for an idealistic objective with which we may not agree.

It is useful to establish a base of definitions.

Data equates to fragments of, or complete facts, that on their own may be insignificant. Data is analog, or digital, and may be numeric, letters, or image. Data are calculated, correlated, and analyzed.

Metadata is data that describes data. Date and time stamps on photography, type, size of an image, when and where the image was created, are metadata. Another example is the time, location, caller, and recipient of a cell telephone call.

A database is a collection of data organized, stored, indexed, and accessed using multiple types of algorithms and program languages and other access tools. For example, Query optimization. Following is a hierarchal structure for an average person. Inquiries are possible from any piece of data.

In theory, everyone contributes to a database, and everyone accesses it for information. The Internet and Google are good examples. In the real world, access to the information in databases is not equal, and there are no controls over where it resides. Actually, using the cloud, information may exist in pieces on disparate computer systems anywhere in the world.

Information is the result of putting data into a useful form, or product. Your home address, for example, is data, but combined with city and state, it is a precise identifiable location.

While information was available in some form prior to the computer age, communicating it was relatively slow. Consistent with Moore's Law, the information world today is pervasive, with a myriad of devices capturing and processing data of every type. Businesses and individuals have the ability to transmit large volumes of data/information anywhere in the world, and/or interact with business and each other in real-time.

Mobile technology has moved the information reality from the office to the world, from voice to image and text, from status to content rich streaming flows. Actionable information is real-time and social media such as Facebook or Linked-In enables global collaboration. The differences between hand-held devices and PCs have blurred, separated more by personal choice and ease of use than functionality. Miniaturized cameras, incorporated in multiple devices, enable the proliferation of images. The technologies as applied to business or personal applications are equally pervasive.

Data ranges from fragments to sets of facts that individually may be insignificant. Data is analog or digital, and may be alphanumeric or image. Data are calculated, correlated, analyzed, and distributed. Data, when pulled together in logical, comprehensive form, is information.

Rules list the conditions to match against the information, which is fed into the program performing the analysis. If it matches the rules, it continues to the next factor. If not, it flags a mismatch and moves to the subsequent calculation or goes to the end of the process. When the analysis is complete, the results are an automated decision of yes, no, reject, or table.

Big data requires massive storage capacity and easy access from anywhere in the world. It is not realistic to carry a computer with enough storage to conduct business and personal affairs. As individuals, we have big data problems as real to our situations as they are to business and governmental organizations. We also want access to every database available, for our own use and advantage. The cloud serves the purpose.

Analytics

Analytics or intelligent software employing artificial intelligence (AI), expert knowledge or other mathematics based computer models tap the power of the database. Enterprises of all types, including governments at every level have embraced the use of analytics. These come in a variety of sizes and shapes from simple drill down to complex AI applications. The objective is to have functionality that builds information products-visualization, decision support, sales analysis, etc. in a timely and trustworthy fashion.

There are thousands of databases capturing and storing information on every type of activity. Of prime concern to this paper are the IRS, health care records, the browsing history on Google and other search engines, and the emergence of powerful and extremely useful geographic tools.

The commercial world

The consumer world has changed, with more of the action moving to the Internet. Business-to-customer (B2C) and business-to-business (B2B) applications are escalating. Every transaction on the internet leaves a traceable footprint back to the buyer. These footprints are collected as both real data, such as purchase orders, names, bank codes, etc., and metadata.

Collectively, these create a condition labeled "big data." Retailers, government, and health care organizations are capturing large volumes of real-time data from multiple sources, including   enterprise, vendors, patients, and customers. Where the prior evolutions of technology left business and government searching for viable analytical data, the problem today is how to manage and convert these large data into useful information products.

Decision-making programs, based on artificial intelligence (AI) or expert systems, collectively called analytics, have application throughout society. Most of these augment decisions, with humans controlling the final decision, but analytics also allows action without an interface.

The following chart illustrates the concepts of predictive analytics.

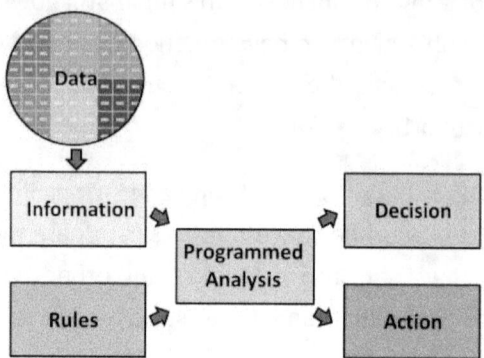

Enterprises of every type are working on integration and automation in some form. There may be opportunities for sharing solutions, especially in the arena of information technology.

The cloud

Cloud computing, a misnomer but a useful term, defines storage and processing solutions. Gartner defines cloud computing as "a style of computing in which scalable and elastic IT-enabled capabilities are delivered as a service using Internet technologies." Cloud service providers have massive or shared computer power and storage, paid for by subscription or amount of service used. These include multi-tenant service bureaus, and all web based processing, such as Software as a Service (SaaS), Service Oriented Architecture (SOA), and Application Service Provider (ASP), under the cloud umbrella.

The tools exist to integrate most systems and databases. The issue is cost, time, and result. The problems are the differences in format, field sizes, formulas used, programming language, and database technology. Each system is dissimilar in size and calculation, and conversion is required to move between systems. The reconciliation of these issues is basic to any form of automated integration, but the mashed result may introduce greater error than its parts.

Software code, defining how data will be processed and put into useful information, is relatively static. Modifications can be complicated and expensive. The term flexible information system means a set of tightly designed and written procedures for executing repetitive formulas, with designed-in flexibility through coding structures and functionality. Adaptive, contemporary systems use Apps of virtually every type.

While focusing primarily on the negative aspects of large integrated databases, some types of large systems are necessities. Comprehensive geo-information systems such as ESRI will insure our future survival. ESRI stands for Environmental Systems Research Institute.

Geospatial processing

ERSI is the most comprehensive geo-information company in the world. Their products are Geographic Information Systems (GIS), and geo database management applications. They can literally map the world and every feature about it, by fractions of an inch, for land use applications.

These geophysical databases also contain the underground infrastructure and data needed to maintain the streets, fireplugs, electrical service, natural gas, cable television, etc. Tied to local tax data, these databases provide a comprehensive representation of the people living in the home, the value of the home, its construction, lot size- in other words, not just images but relevant information.

Extending the concept, farmers can literally obtain an inch-by-inch visualization and analysis of soil content. Using high-technology equipment, production optimization occurs for each inch. This involves the precise application of fertilizer and other soil enhancers, along with precise amounts of water as needed. (See the Advanced Agriculture presentation on CompetitiveAmerica.us). The technology has enormous benefits for managing natural and renewable resources. The functionally will enable huge gains in agricultural yields, warn of geophysical problems, and achieve optimal transportation routes. Geo information is gathered and used to increase harvest and conservation of ocean resources. Human imagination, creativity, and innovation are the only limits to the applications.

The problem, merging disparate databases multiples the potential for mischief, larceny, and coercion.

Health Care

The Affordable Care Act (ACA) created a de facto national health care database. While it does not necessarily include personal health care data, in conformity with HIPAA 5010, it is comprised of codes and metadata. EMR/EHR records form an enormous share of the new quality standard in the ACA, and the completion of electronic records establishes the base for compensation. They have also proved to be prime targets for cybercriminals.

Every person receiving medical care will have services and conditions recorded in broad and extensive detail. Its use represents a two-edged sword. Striking with one edge, data will be available to help manage health care quality and focus on emerging issues. The federal governing board will use these data for service level decisions. Decisions on health care will be statistical and discriminate against certain medical conditions where the cost may not justify life-supporting treatment. In these cases, the sword slices the other direction.

The major concern in any application is data accuracy. The old acronym, GIGO, or garbage in, garbage out, has frightening implications for patient care. For these reasons, it is always wise to check every medical document that you get for accuracy, and make sure the provider corrects all errors.

Your digital clone

Medical personnel created your information clone when they filled out your birth certificate. The data piled up geometrically, with education records, athletic and scholastic awards, newspapers, a brand new social security number, jobs, military record, business affiliations, tax records, internet surfing practices, where you worked, and how long, and sometimes even personal performance. In recent years, postings on Facebook, and other social media - literally any digital and savable information added to the compilations.

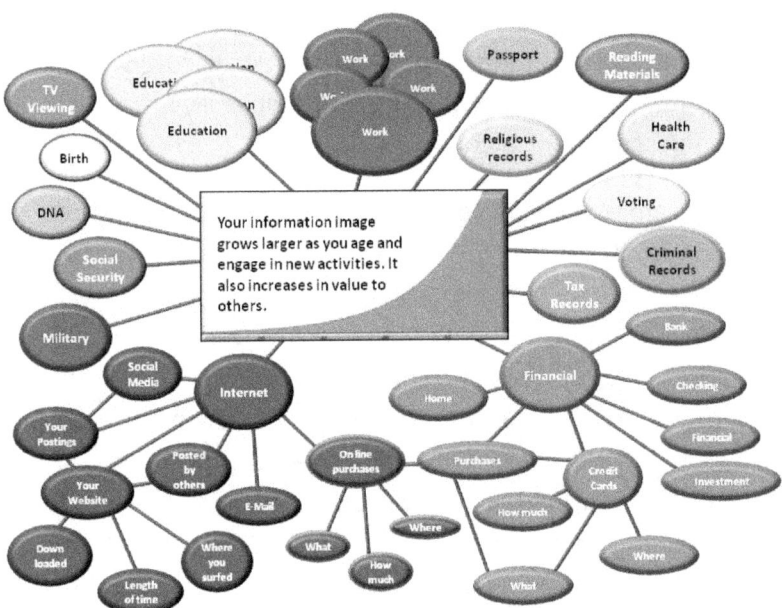

When we marry, our database suddenly increases, and the data for each member added to that of all the others.

Each child further expands the database

Nearly all stores, of all types, record and digitize every movement, and there are cameras on many streets. People randomly (or knowingly) take our photographs in virtually every environment, and given the size and stealth characteristics of recording equipment, we will never know it. Devices are available to track our cars, and to record every word uttered anywhere.

Currently, a tremendous amount of accumulated data exists about you and those you care for. It is located in an unknown number of disparate databases. Every demographic is targeted with commercial information, including suggested purchases and political messaging. In truth, all are subject to highly intrusive privacy violations increasing the data collected about each of us. Remarkably, even if we live a pure, boring, mundane existence and never worry about blackmail, loved ones around us may not be clean-living, subjecting all family members to outside influence.

Converging computer technologies provide the data to build information capable of knowing where we are (cell phones), what we are buying (credit card transactions), and sometimes where we are going (Facebook, trip planning on Google or MapQuest). Even in your home, there can be embedded technology in your telephone, computer, television, automobile, or any device using computer chips. It is given that identity theft is pervasive, and we covered this topic in the April Focused Fire Newsletter, Issue 10, posted on CompetitiveAmerica.us and titled "Internet Security and Identity Theft." Unfortunately, this is only the beginning of the mischief possible when the databases are integrated.

This chart illustrates the current situation.

The integration of our health care records into the IRS database is part of the ACA was not to provide better health care. Given Internet search engines provide data to political campaigns, data abuse is already pervasive, but barely scratches the surface of the consequences of a national database, where all these data are integrated.

How information is used

Government and business use information for a variety of commercial and private purposes, for and against citizens/consumers. For this paper, there are two major areas of concern. The first issue is the security of our information, and the second is the overall threat for the media to control and manipulate information to sell us a point of view.

The next chapter discusses the FREE PRESS, and how it is now used against us.

25. The Press

The press - hardcopy, television, and online services, are a pervasive thread running through this book. The media stands out as the greatest disappointment relative to the decline of America. While governmental actions of are destructive, the abdication of the press to the political process has long-term consequences to America's liberty, and strikes at the heart of our trust for the system.

The Framers carved out a special place for a free press, with the intent that it would stand for the people against governmental abuse. Instead, the press has supported the administration on virtually every issue, becoming complicit with the government itself by selectively editing and publishing materials.

To be fair, the press may be the victim of coercion and bullying, but the interbreeding with government is significant. There are marriages and other personal relationships between governmental officials and the press. For example, David Rhodes, CBS News President, is the brother to Ben Rhodes, an Obama adviser. Ben Rhodes made the following statement regarding the attempt by the president to bypass Congress on a nuclear arms agreement with Iran. For the most part, it was unreported.

> "Bottom line is, this is the best opportunity we've had to resolve the Iranian issue diplomatically, certainly since President Obama came to office, and probably since the beginning of the Iraq war," Rhodes said. "So no small opportunity, it's a big deal. This is probably the biggest thing President Obama will do in his second

term on foreign policy. This is healthcare for us, just to put it in context."

Source: "Obama adviser likened Iran nuclear deal to Obama Care," By Matthew Continetti, Published October 31, 2014, Washington Free Beacon

There was a pushback, as the Obama administration increasingly limited and steps on the press.

A renowned investigative reporter, Sharyl Attkisson, who once worked for CBS, has published her memoir, titled <u>Stonewalled: My Fight for Truth Against the Forces of Obstruction, Intimidation, and Harassment in Obama's Washington.</u>

Other media personalities are speaking out about the lack of transparency and manipulation of the press.

Susan Page, the USA Washington Bureau Chief, stated:

> "My big fear is that this administration has been more restrictive and more challenging to the press, more dangerous to the press, really, than any administration in American history in terms of legal investigations and so on. And I think access to the White House has just gotten worse and worse."

> http://newsbusters.org/blogs/melissa-mullins/2014/10/31/usa-todays-susan-page-obama-team-most-dangerous-press-us-history#sthash.aViAStJK.dpuf

It is difficult to feel sorry for the press. While they complain, it will not change their behavior.

Fact: the press prints what the White House provides and ignores the important and controversial issues at the heart of honest governance.

This is a bold statement, and readers are justified for insisting that I "prove it." Here is the proof, in their words.

Ben Rhodes, in mid-May 2016, admitted to misleading the press and the American people to sell the nuclear deal with Iran. It is similar to the manipulation the administration used to sell the Affordable Health Care Act. The following websites provide the details and actual narrative.

> https://www.washingtonpost.com/lifestyle/style/obama-official-says-he-pushed-a-narrative-to-media-to-sell-the-iran-nuclear-deal/2016/05/06/5b90d984-13a1-11e6-8967-7ac733c56f12_story.html

> http://www.nytimes.com/2016/05/08/magazine/the-aspiring-novelist-who-became-obamas-foreign-policy-guru.html?_r=0

> https://whyevolutionistrue.wordpress.com/2016/05/09/journalism-dies-by-a-thousand-cuts-manipulated-by-the-white-house/

The reason, they believe they have all of the intelligence and everyone else is stupid, therefore, any means justifies the end. The Obama administration was determined to complete the agreement as part of the Presidents' legacy.

Of greater importance is for us to understand exactly how they set up a propaganda system to deceive the American public.

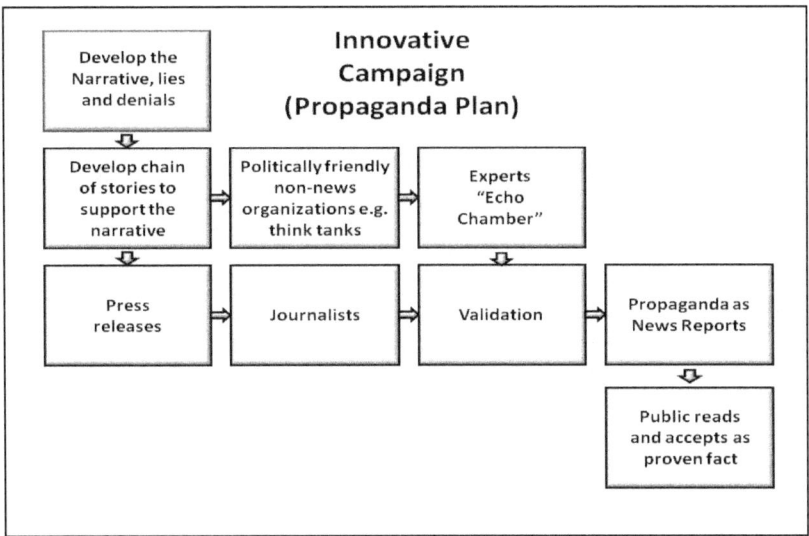

This chart is a visualization of Ben Rhodes words.

The administration, primarily under his direction, developed a narrative supporting the agreement, then lies and denials to explain away every question, concern and time line. To accomplish this required them to know precisely what Americans would reject, and what Congress would push back on. Drilling down, it also meant they knew it was a horrible deal, but jeopardized us anyway. Their real reasons are unknown. What we do know, it was not for our greater good.

The narratives (propaganda) were fed to politically friendly non-news organizations, experts and think tanks that supported the administration, which journalists contacted to verify information. Ben Rhodes called them "echo chambers."

The administration issued press releases (propaganda) to journalists, many of them young and inexperienced, who validated the information by contacting the experts who echoed the administrations narrative, lies, and denials.

The press publishes the reports for our consumption. We either accept it as fact, or Google the sources that echoed the misinformation for validation.

When congress attempted to call Mr. Rhodes to account, the White House refused to allow him to testify.

Given this insight, the deceptions involved with the Affordable Care Act are obvious.

The press upon which the public once relied for honest reporting apparently abdicated responsibility in reporting the ACA, either buying the "any means" argument, or were so deeply bias the truth was invisible. Perhaps there was also an echo chamber.

Frequently, dishonesty in the press is omission, sitting on information needed by the public to make evidence-based decisions. While researching our book Productivity Prescriptions for Health Care, Jon Bingol and I had little difficulty finding and anticipating the major flaws in the ACA, and extrapolating the considerable consequences. Largely ignored, the issues still must approach the crisis stage before coverage by the mainstream press. When the 2017 rate and deductibles are announced, the truth about the program will become apparent.

In defense of the press, no one wants to listen to the problems. In my personal bias, the modern press was absorbed into, and then abdicated to the political process, failing its role to keep the public honestly informed.

The concerns over information integrity continue to intensify. We all must understand, there are no guardians at the door.

The following chart breaks information use into four categories, starting with knowledge, and progressing into social control. Somewhere between propaganda and control, the free press disappears, compromising all personal freedoms and rights. The process can be so subtle that society in general may not realize it has occurred until it is a fait accompli.

The Four Stages of Information Control

1. Knowledge "As it is"

A free press dedicated to finding and reporting the truth. One that will fight government attempts to control access or manipulate facts. Ability of individuals to manage personal data.

2. Propaganda "How we want you to see it"

Opportunist manipulation of, or denial of facts to press and media. A complicit media moves propaganda closer to social programming. Business and government use of personal data collected from a variety of sources for targeting.

3. Programming "What we want you to do"

Limit what, when, how, and where content is controlled to reinforce bias (path most traveled).
Access to all personal data, control of the media, and corrupted governmental agencies. Privacy no longer exists.

4. Control "Do what we tell you"

Information is managed by the government and used to coerce, intimidate, or otherwise control the populace. Medical care can be withheld, cronyism prevails. Free enterprise is dead. This type of society is labeled **dystopian**.

The media can/does cooperate with government to deliver political messages precisely to the consumer. These situations are evolving into propaganda and programming," to control what we do.

Check off where you think America is at on this chart, then put an arrow, down or up, for the direction you believe the country is heading. Then ask our question again -**WHY?**

In his book, <u>Nineteen Eighty-Four</u>, George Orwell described a dystopian world called Oceania, where the government controlled everything through the collection and manipulation of information.

What we can do

There are steps we can take to guard against propaganda and programming. Unfortunately, if we allow ourselves to fall through to the last block, control, the only options are obedience or revolution.

We gather information in small chunks, and it is important to question the validity of every input.

Be aware that we are all biased, and by nature tend to consume information reinforcing those opinions. Try to expand the input base and question the relationships of information.

We rely on expert and group opinion. These sources may be wrong, or manipulated into a course of action.

Be constantly on guard when told to do something for the "greater good." Who established what it means and why should it drive our actions?

From a macro perspective, we need to vote for candidates that actually represent our best interests, and hold them accountable. The freedoms of future generations depend on what we do today.

Avoid thrashing ignorance

Thrashing ignorance (The Ladder of Inference) is a wasteful and universal process that most of us engage in periodically. It means stacking up assumptions as if they are valid facts, then adding dialog, debating the issue, and defining a solution. None of it is real, and it does not require knowledge. Ignorance is the lack of knowledge, and the process perpetuates the ignorance. The problem occurs when we accept the false premises as facts, and put them into action.

Here is how it works.

Someone brings up a problem or situation, real or implied. Participants feed assumptions into the discussion. Others add opinions, sometimes-real facts, often making it more real. Frequently, the debate over solutions is intense and emotional, until reaching agreement.

The consequence is an **assumed solution for an assumed problem**.

Thrashing ignorance is deeply rooted in the workplace and society in general. The repetitious nature of major news channels daily reinforces the concept.

Government feeds and perpetuates the process because individual's busy thrashing ignorance is not seeking the truth. The solution is to test for assumption or fact, and if non-productive, stop doing it.

Properly define problems and situations. Get the facts and test them for accuracy and truth, making it possible to define implementable solutions to real problems.

Question EVERYTHING the press and government tell you. You know they have lied extensively in the past, and maintaining control over us, the sheep, means they will keep doing it.

26. *China*

Photo: Wayne Staley

I congratulate all of you, my fellow Americans. We have succeeded in achieving the inconceivable. It is so preposterous, that twenty years ago I would have laughed at the thought. Unfortunately, humor is missing in action. In any event, it is a self-imposed agony with enormous consequences. Worse, our children and grandchildren will ultimately pay the price.

While Americans looked inwards, engaged in politics between Democrats and Republicans, the consequences of redistribution and downsizing are now real and absolute. China is the new world's Number

One Superpower. They surpassed the United States in late 2014, in industrial output and Gross Domestic Product (GDP), by adjusted Purchasing Power Parity (PPP), measuring actual outputs on an equivalent basis.

The numbers tell the story. The first set is money reinvested back into the economy. While America invested only 1.85% of GDP, less than the rate of inflation, China invested heavily, 8.04% to grow their country. Countries, like individuals, that fail to invest resources for the future will ultimately wind up on the short end of the stick. In addition, our National debt is projected to grow. China owns a big chunk of that debt, and the banker is not always kind to the debtor.

Economic Indicators: Investment (% of GDP) 2013 -Billions USD

	GDP Unadjusted	% Reinvested
China	$9,020.31	8.04%
United States	$16,237.75	1.85%

http://www.economywatch.com/economic-statistics/

The second set of numbers shows industrial production for the United States and China. Ten years ago, China's output was less than 50% of the USA it is now 50% larger. This growth was the result of deliberately dismantling our economy and transferring it to China.

Industrial Production By Country

Country	Level Ind Prod	Units	As Of	1Y Chg	~5Y Ago	~10Y Ago
USA	3,054.53	Billion USD	2013	2.88%	2,620.05	2,826.54
China	4,008.35	Billion USD	2013	9.70%	2,529.54	1,262.09

https://www.quandl.com/c/economics/industrial-production-by-country

We normally compare economies based on GDP (above), and using this measurement the United States is economically far ahead of China. This is +the delusion of numbers. A far better, but more controversial measurement is Purchasing Power Parity, defined as:

> "An economic theory that estimates the amount of adjustment needed on the exchange rate between countries in order for the exchange to be equivalent to each currency's purchasing power." (http://www.investopedia.com/terms/p/ppp.asp)

Using this measurement, sometime during 2014, China passed the United States in both output and national wealth.

Chinese cybercrime

China continually hacks into every American system. China unveiled the Shenyang J-31 Falcon Eagle, a direct clone of the U.S. Joint Strike Fighter, while President Obama was visiting China. America spent billions of dollars developing the fifth-generation fighter, but the Chinese can market theirs as a low-cost alternative, in competition against U.S. manufacturers. Our government will remain silent.

Industry and consumers alike have become accustomed to hacking attacks. The litany involves Heartland Payment Systems, TJX Companies Inc., Epsilon, Department of Veterans Affairs, Sony PlayStation Network, ESTsoft, AOL, Target and the list goes on. The accumulative effect is millions of personal records potentially hacked with immeasurable consequences, but certainly amounting to billions of dollars.

Unfortunately, the attacks have been taking a turn to the darker side. In 2009, the Chinese government attacked Google, Yahoo and other Internet companies. The government gathered data on Chinese human rights leaders, and appropriated intellectual property.

Coercion at a personal level is the new and the most insidious form.

If the Chinese can hack into every other database, why not the National database of you and me?

Perhaps North Korea beat them to it.

Sony

Sony Entertainment produced a comedy titled "The Interview," starring James Franco and Seth Rogen. The plot is an assassination attempt against Kim Jong Un, the supreme leader of North Korea. From all appearances, the Koreans fail to find the film humorous. They reportedly launched a cyber attack against Sony.

Readers need to view this as a dark omen for the future, when the personal National database is complete, everyone can be controlled and manipulated through coercion, reward, and punishment if/when-governmental agencies exploit our information.

A bleak competitive future

Like it or not, money is power, and over the next five years, projections indicate that China will incrementally gain economic, military, and world power. Each year, our influence will shrink, and eventually become ineffective. At that point, the United States will lose control of future decisions and consequences, and become another failed experiment of democracy.

Our leaders have succeeded in redistributing and downsizing America, and this process continues unabated. Busy squabbling with each other, we ignored the approaching danger, and therefore, participated in the outcome. Arguments about big government or small, free-market or socialist, become useless concepts when liberties are lost. At the point of diminishing return (unable to sustain ourselves), there will be a new reality, whatever China wants it to be.

To those ignoring the consequences of a supreme China, I recommend studying their history. China calls their country the middle kingdom, the center of the universe, and they control the universe. There are no examples of true democracy in their history. The Chinese are hungry for wealth and power, and job formation is critical to the control of the populace. They have waited a long time to reach this point in history, and will do everything to advance the opportunity.

The following quote from "Freedom and Opportunity" sums up our challenge.

> "Immersed in divisive social issues of race and political party, and split among ourselves, our focus is on the wrong priorities. We need to fix our economy, strengthen our position in global competition, and grow the economy to provide jobs and opportunities for every American. China is our enemy, ISIS is our enemy, and poverty is our enemy. Most Americans will agree - my neighbor, regardless of race, religion, political party, gender, or place in society, IS NOT MY ENEMY."

China just passed the U.S. in industrial output, and their continued predatory practices are draining our economy. Their harsh and long-term currency manipulation makes it difficult for American manufacturers to compete. In addition, China steals our intellectual property rights with impunity. Between China and a wasteful government, of both parties, we are $18 trillion dollars in debt, more than one year of our GDP.

Part Five - Fix It Political

27. Your Choice - Policy or Opportunity Driven Society

Life in a Policy Driven Society

For the past seven years, Americans have experienced life in a policy driven, dependency economy where the government exercises ever-tighter constraints while dodging responsibility and discouraging transparency. Labeled "the new normal," the myth of "for the greater good" perpetuates this economic malaise.

America voted twice for this economic model. In 2008, they voted in the Democratic Party, led by President Barack Obama. In 2012, in spite of a poorly performing economy and dishonest governance, they voted to renew his efforts.

The net result of the last seven years is a country and world that emulates the president. Trust is a rare commodity, and virtually no one believes what President Obama says. This distrust has brought the normal flow of governing to a halt, and slashed American's influence and strength in the global arena.

America needs to rebuild an opportunity society, where hard work and effort pay off for the individual and society in general. An opportunity society is free market based, but differs from capitalism or laissez faire on two important points. First, the concept does not support the exploitation of labor, capital, and resources for pure monetary gain. A clean environment and personal freedoms are prerequisites. Second, it does not reject the regulations required to prevent systemic abuse.

194

At the same time, in an opportunity society, government cannot exploit business, labor, capital, and resources to achieve unrealistic or artificial economic parity. It is not free to implement transformational programs, by any name, without the consent of the people. Government cannot use its position to justify and/or achieve dystopian objectives. When it attempts to do so, historically, it actually increases the overall waste through the cost of government and the inefficiencies implicit in "big bureaucratic systems," while wreaking lasting damage to our freedoms.

It would be easy to drift into an idealistic discussion, defining unworkable concepts, but from a systems perspective, all ideas and actions must spring from the same thought and effort, with pragmatic application. To achieve these purposes requires a clear and practical description of an "opportunity driven society." First, we must construct some conceptual foundation.

Basic forms of governance

There are two fundamental organizational structures, hierarchal and self-organizing.

The traditional organizational structure is a hierarchy.

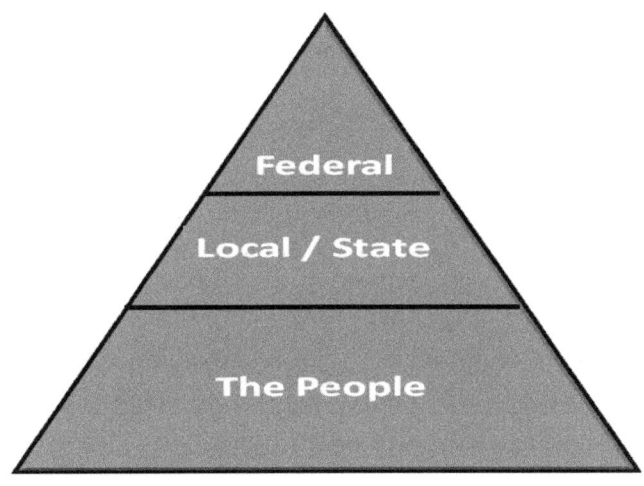

The upper tier is independent (causal), and all the other layers are dependent (effect). Power is concentrated at the top and distributed by direction and control through the layers within the organization, with the expectation that all will agree and comply with the directive. Failure is interpreted as insubordination and the penalties are sometimes severe.

Hierarchal forms of government include dictatorships, monarchies, socialism, and dystopia. In these structures, the term equality and hierarchy are an oxymoron. A hierarchy controls and distributes power and wealth down through a dependent constituency and promotes a greater good, often meaning whatever goals the bureaucracy needs to sustain its power or reach its objectives.

The government determines which freedoms the people can enjoy, with wealth and resources managed directly or through regulatory mechanisms. Bureaucrats choose which laws to enforce, and which legal violations to investigate or tolerate, and the government avoids accountability by manipulating or controlling information. The government has the power over the people, who are accountable to the government. The government rewards those who support its actions, and punishes those that do not.

The tiers within a hierarchy take many forms, but equality is not one of them. Pick up the business section of any newspaper and it is apparent the rich are benefiting from the stock market. The poor are increasingly supported by public assistance, and the middle class is shrinking. It seems obvious, but this type of redistribution and downsizing of America is resulting in a poorer, inequitable economy and society by design of our own federal government.

Complexity occurs because many activities within a hierarchy are not dependent. Persons responsible for achieving the delegated tasks have free thought and independent action. Hierarchies incorrectly assume shared values and purpose. Each level filters directives, and people may not choose to execute them. Sometimes, the metrics failed to hold them accountable, but more frequently they do not see any reason to do it or believe it harmful. People have different agendas, perspectives, and knowledge. Every person makes decisions daily that affect varying degrees of performance.

Self-organizing—the second concept partially originates in complex adaptive theory. In summary, it states that all groups of people develop their own culture, beliefs, and sets of values. They select leaders, and perform work to self-determined standards. Natural work groups are rooted in this concept. Actually, self-organizing groups flourish even within hierarchies. The problem is when they take action contrary to the directions given from the top.

Democracy and Federalism are special examples of self-organizing systems. The people set the policies and elect an abbreviated form of hierarchy to govern. The purpose is the common good, such as protection, administration of laws, and faithful and equal promotion of the best societal interests. In a democracy, the people determine "the greater good," and government helps the people achieve those objectives. Conflicted, Americans are partially operating under both forms of government, and many suffer from political schizophrenia.

It is remarkable, given the opportunity to be king, that George Washington refused, aware that the secret to a successful country was free people. He and the other founders established a miracle of governance that continues until this day. In our form of government, the people have the final say. The people elect the appropriate local and state governments, granting them the primary authority to do the peoples will. That is, pass and enforce laws, build roads and structures, provide education, and in general, provide for the collective needs of the people.

America has a federal government to establish laws over the collection of states. Under the Constitution, it has only the power delegated by the states. The primary mission of centralized government is protecting the citizens and enforcing the freedoms guaranteed by the Constitution. In this structure, the power remains with the people, per the following illustration. In the parallel illustration, freedoms equate to structure. As long as the people have the power, they retain all the freedoms.

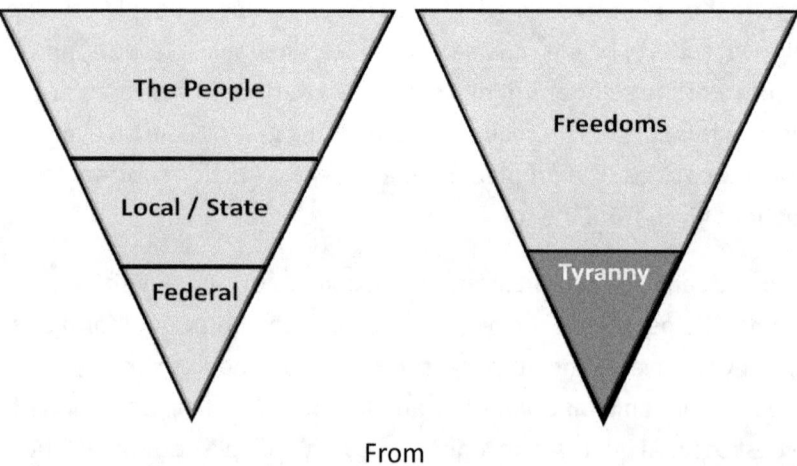

From

These guiding principles are under attack, as our current leaders attempt to flip the country from, "<u>we</u> the people," to "<u>me</u> the government." We must not deceive ourselves, both parties are complicit in the effort to divide the people and share the spoils. The difference is that President Obama provides leadership to people that have demonstrated their mission - to change America through the mechanisms of redistribution and downsizing, powered by a policy driven, top-down system.

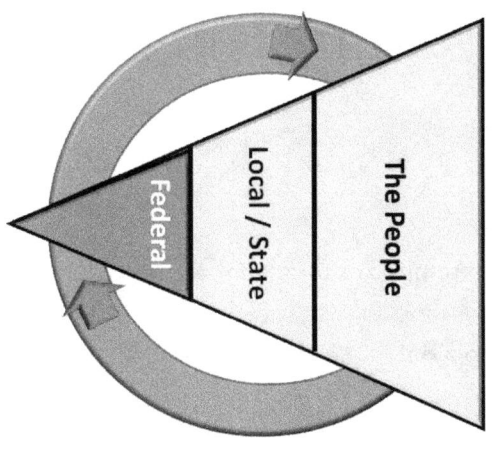

To

These two perspectives dictate different responses and governing styles. Hierarchical systems are directing while self-organizing systems imply enabling. Hierarchal systems are not democratic, and the power always accumulates at the top. History teaches us lessons, among them the sad truth that forfeited freedoms do not come back.

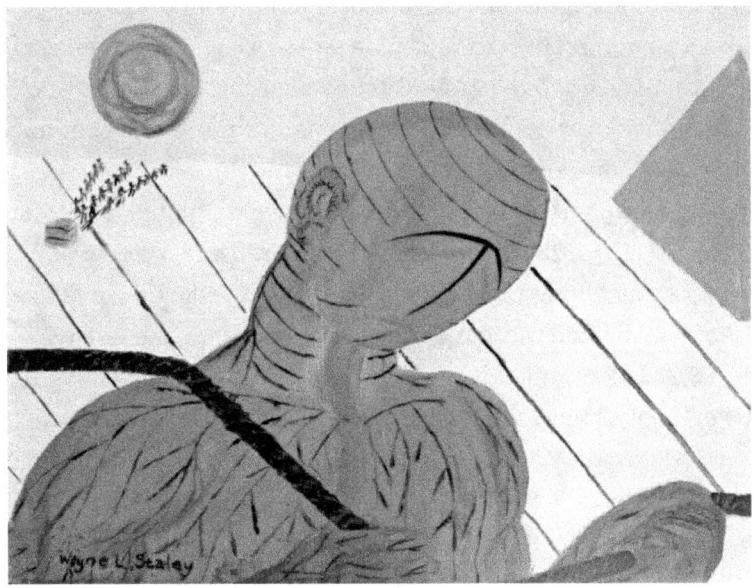

28 Political Solutions

When the voters attempt to alter an entrenched course, in this case, the direction America is heading, but repeatedly fail, the result is frustration. If people riot in the streets and burn buildings, that is anger.

Frustration

The genesis for our unhappy state occurred at the nexus of two disruptive, fractured continuums. It started in mid-1950 with the civil rights movement, and ended in 1975 with the conclusion of the Vietnam War. Both generated true anger, scarring our political process. The civil rights issue continues to fester, but Vietnam cut a deep, still unabridged, political chasm.

On August 2, 1964, North Vietnamese torpedo boats attacked the U.S. destroyer Maddox in the Gulf of Tonkin, and repeated (reportedly) the attack two days later. It was the beginning of a long, undeclared war. Our government lied to the American people regarding the status of the conflict. Vietnam was the first war where people received a continuous feed of images showing the horrors, such as My Lai. Kill count replaced meaningful metrics of progress. College campuses erupted in protest, and on May 4, 1970, 28 National guardsmen fired into a crowd of protesters at Kent State University in Ohio, killing four and wounding nine. Vietnam marked the loss of American innocence and civility. Worse, 58,220 of our military died, and for those returning home, injured or whole, fellow Americans unfairly vilified them all as baby-killers.

Starting in 1969, the Social Security Trust Fund was included in the unified budget, allowing the Federal government to deplete the SS trust fund to pay for the undeclared and unbudgeted war by using "IOUs." The Vietnam conflict and the raid on SS occurred on the democrats watch, under Presidents John Kennedy and Lyndon Johnson. President Richard Nixon, a republican, escalated the conflict until events like Kent State University turned most of the country against the war, then he unceremoniously withdrew all American military, as North Vietnamese troops occupied Saigon.

On the upper shelf in my study is a dusty book titled "The Watergate Papers." It chronicles the 1972 escapades of a Republican team breaking into the Democratic National Committee Headquarters in Washington, D.C. Voters knew about the break-in before the election, but Republicans and independents ignored the problem, electing President Nixon.

Reviewing the chain of presidents is enlightening.

Lyndon B Johnson, after depleting Social Security and micro managing the Vietnam War, chose not to run for re-election. The Watergate cover-up eventually led to Nixon's resignation. The people refused to re-elect George H W Bush because he committed to a no-tax policy, and broke his promise. President Bill Clinton, while not convicted, went through an embarrassing impeachment process and the government was grid locked.

George W Bush presided over people divided and angry about the wars in Afghanistan and Iraq. They viewed the former as a necessary response to the 911 attacks on New York City. Then he invaded Iraq, overthrowing Saddam Hussein without an exit strategy. We felt betrayed when the developmental processes for making atom weapons proved unfounded.

In 2008, the voters elected Barack Obama, who promised fundamental change in the American system. For the most part, he has achieved that commitment, significantly changing social systems while ignoring economic growth. Americans, now understanding the mismatch between his objectives and theirs, are not all pleased.

Like Nixon, Obama pulled out of the wars, but the consequences were very different. Leaving Vietnam hurt our pride, while the withdrawal from Iraq and Afghanistan created a void filled by radical Islamist groups, a threat to the United States.

Although it has received insufficient press attention, President Obama and Hillary Clinton precipitated the overthrow of Gaddafi in Libya, leaving that country in chaos. The Obama administration, including Hillary Clinton, birthed and nurtured ISIS. It was the perfect setup for the radicals to burn the American consulate, resulting in four deaths, including J Christopher Stevens, the American ambassador.

The President apparently believes the United States is a world economic and political bully, and must learn to play nicely with others by conceding hard-earned fortune, power, and territory. He opened the door for ruthless bullies like Iran, ISIS, Russia, and North Korea, who want to take us out in a street fight. Like all bullies, they will gang up to get the job done, and then again fight among themselves.

Citizens opposed the President's policies and executive orders, but when they voted the Republicans into majority status in both houses, nothing changed. It was positive proof of a system rigged against the average citizen.

Corrupted systems

Dominated by special interests, there is little room for executing the will of the people. Nothing changes because that would mean disrupting the lives of those comfortably occupying the bureaucracy. Over time, every human system rots from the inside and is unable to perform the intended purpose. It exists to self-perpetuate until eventually collapsing or the people revolt and replace it.

A Broken Justice System

The parallel to the Nixon Watergate is on hold, as FBI Director James Comey appeared to indict Hillary Clinton, and then proclaimed a "lack of evidence." All occurred just days after Pres. Bill Clinton met in private with Loretta Lynch, the Attorney General.

This, for most of the country, was absolute evidence of America's two-tier justice system. Like Watergate, however, much of the evidence is undiscovered, but may well reach critical mass after the election.

Class distinction is one of the first signs of a government too corrupted to self-correct. The rule of law punishes people who sell cigarettes on the street, but allow politicians who expose national secrets and let our Ambassadors die, to run for President.

The government that wants our guns releases undocumented alien criminals into the populace, and through the Fast and Furious program, gave powerful 50-caliber rifles to the Mexican drug cartel.

The government disrespects law enforcement, but gives mass amnesty to criminals. It attempts to repeal the second amendment by executive action, making gun ownership and self-protection difficult to impossible.

The government releases terrorists from Guantanamo, and spends millions to target them with drones.

Finally, the Supreme Court has proven it has forgotten its mission, to uphold the Constitution. Justice Ruth Bader Ginsburg took a political position against one of the Presidential candidates. If that candidate becomes president, how can the Supreme Count be impartial? If her choice for President is elected, how does the court avoid future conflicts of interest?

The next President will name three or more Justices, and the stakes are extremely high. The integrity of the Constitution of the United States and its principles of freedom are on the line. Stated differently, YOUR freedoms are in jeopardy.

Apprehensive (Concerned)

Fear is both a noun and a verb, but in either form, it implies dangers and threats to personal or family health or resources. It can be extreme, where we run, hide, or fight back. It may also be apprehension, where we are aware of the dangers, and willing to take steps to avoid worst-case scenarios. The economy is virtually stagnant, and Americans are apprehensive of their future and the future of their children.

The Social Security liability has reached 14.7 trillion dollars while the retired population grows, and the number of worker's declines. People paying into SS today have little confidence the program will be there for them. Meanwhile, governmental employees are guaranteed lucrative retirement benefits. For 2016, Federal employees, theoretically using the same COLA formula as the one for Social Security, will get a raise, while SS recipients will not. How did this happen? Congress turned their heads and pretended not to see the situation, and did nothing. Congress voted for the Affordable Health Care Act, and the President exempted them from compliance. When it was time to correct the situation, by Congress voting to apply the law equally to federal employees, Rand Paul led a coalition to kill the effort and head off the embarrassment of a vote. The act of making Congress and its employees above the law was clearly a double standard.

Americans are apprehensive about the hypocrisy of government, its lack of response to the complex problems, the effect of its actions on liberty, the economy, and safety. The intended purpose of the Federal government is keeping the people safe. Twisted along the way, the new purpose is perpetuating a growing bureaucracy.

Bureaucracy

The pendulum swings back and forth from Democrat to Republican, but nothing changes. Given the turnover in government, a person would think that somewhere we would find civility and a government doing the right thing for the right reasons. However, it seems that nothing really gets better. There is a reasonable but troubling explanation.

America has all the assets needed to build an opportunity society for every citizen, but government does not even have a plan to fix the problem. The disadvantaged in our society, including much of the black community, are promised help by every administration, but there are fewer opportunities and more poverty than before. Meanwhile, government opens the doors for illegal immigrants who compete for the same resources. In our net sum society, most groups lose, except those in government or other entrenched bureaucracies.

Americans are not insane, angry, or fearful. They are frustrated, apprehensive, and looking for a solution to nagging economic and international problems. They are tired of the hypocrisy and the politicians who perpetuate a corrupted system. That often-used quote credited to Einstein is appropriate. "Insanity is doing the same thing over and over again and expecting different results."

A time for decision

Decisions based on a fact-driven process increase the ability to choose between multiple options. Decision Making in a Disruptive Reordering.

All options have variables, and the more complex the subject, the greater the number of variables. That translates into working harder to get the appropriate facts needed to make a good decision. The Presidential election is in November. Emotions decided the last two elections, and this time voters need to get the facts.

There are different sets of questions that every voter needs to ask and answer. The first are personal attributes regarding the candidates.

- ☐ Will they focus efforts on their first Constitutional responsibility, to protect the homeland?
- ☐ Will they listen to the will of the people or act through executive authority?
- ☐ Are they fit to be the commander in chief?
- ☐ Have they demonstrated the qualities of leadership?
- ☐ Will they uphold the Constitution and Bill of Rights of the United States of America?
- ☐ Will they enforce the laws of the land?
- ☐ Are they passionate about America and our future?
- ☐ Are they honest and can the electorate trust them to take positive actions to enable prosperity?
- ☐ Do they have a record of real accomplishments?
- ☐ Will they put words into action?
- ☐ Can they deal with the complicated issues of our advanced, technological society?
- ☐ Are they strong enough to stand up for America in the global economy?
- ☐ Are they in debt to any foreign entity?

The second set of questions relates to policy.

- ☐ Do they have a vision for a prosperous American future for all citizens?
- ☐ Do they know how to get it done?
- ☐ How will they grow the economy while protecting the environment?
- ☐ What is their posture on national defense?
- ☐ What will they do about immigration?

The Constitution is clear, and the following are factors of equality, not electability. None affects the intellect or leadership capability of the individuals. Disqualify any candidate using them. Our president and other political leaders are responsible to all the people. Period.

- ☐ Race
- ☐ Sex
- ☐ Religion

American citizens will go to the polls this November. Failure to cast a ballot is the equivalent to a yes for the Obama agenda. We have a personal choice. I will vote just as much against the Obama/Clinton agenda as for a Republican, then start on the newly elected officials to build an opportunity driven society.

Sadly, if I base the future on the past, Americans will not overcome bias, nor get the facts, and may well make a decision they later regret. Like the students at Britexit, the young people will hit Google, looking for the answers they needed BEFORE the vote.

Four years from now, we will again say "enough," look in the mirror to find the reason, to see Einstein's smiling image. Then look outward to contemplate our arrival in Ayn Rand's dystopia, where the new politically incorrect word is "I." There are no individuals, only components of the bureaucracy.

Part Six - Fix It Economic

29. *The Zone of Opportunity*

The ESC (escape) button on a computer keyboard allows the user to cancel the current process. On November 4, 2014, the American people hit the political ESC key, voting against the Obama administration agenda.

The Election Results

The election was the result of two forces. One was the incentivized Republicans, and the other a distrust of the president and the rejection of his policies. The Republicans, with majorities in both the House and the Senate, offered few positive plans to move the country forward.

The new Republican legislators gave President Obama everything he asked for. The election was a waste of taxpayer money and time.

What the people want

The election was about the concerns of the American people; most believe we are far from agreement on direction. Searching for answers, we analyzed numerous polls. Democrats and Republicans have different priorities, but the major issues are on both lists

One of the polls ranked the problems as:

1 Safety
2 Unemployment
3 Dissatisfaction with government/congress/politicians: poor leadership/corruption/abuse of power
4 Economy
5 Health Care
6 Government debt

Conspicuously missing from all the lists is global competition.

Presidential Reaction

The Presidents response to the recent election was to ignore the results, immediately issuing executive orders to implement an immigration program.

The immigration issue is disruptive, diversionary, and serves President Obama's purpose. While everyone looks at the diversion, he is proceeding without restraints on his primary objective. To use the considerable bureaucracy at his disposal to fundamentally, and obsessively, restructure America. Weakened economically, socially, militarily, and as a global power, he continued to downsize, redistribute, and dilute America. It is obviously his intent to do so as long as he has the power to shape policies and actions. He has demonstrated the intent to push the powers of the office to the edge of, and beyond its limits.

President Obama is using executive powers to tighten Environmental Protection Agency (EPA) regulations, and impose other regulatory constraints. He is taking highly contentious actions to force his ideals on the country. Congress is doing little to oppose it.

Immersed in divisive social issues of race and political party, and split among ourselves, the focus is on the wrong priorities.

The 2016 election has shown high levels of dissatisfaction between the governed and the governing. The rupturing of traditional political parties may signal the beginning of a new political structure in America. It appears the people are demonstrating their displeasure through the ballot box, and the bureaucrats in both parties are concerned.

Regardless of politics, we need to fix our economy, strengthen our position in global competition, and grow the economy to provide jobs and opportunities for every American.

Response

The Framers carefully constructed the balance of government between the executive, legislative, and judicial branches to guard against executive over-reach. They designed the system to respond slowly and deliberately to prevent excessive action and reaction. Recent rulings have converted the court into a third legislative body. The three-part American system has lost equilibrium.

For that reason, America is in imminent danger. Citizens are becoming increasingly aware of the magnitude of the changes, and the potential consequences of redistribution, downsizing, unilateral actions, and presidential over- reach, all supported by an activist judicial system.

States, legislators and businesses have filed lawsuits on immigration and the ACA. The judicial system has been slow to react to an executive over-reach and reluctant to reverse legislation, e.g. rulings dealing with the ACA. For that reason, the courts impact is uncertain.

The Rule of Law in America is very tenuous, and the evolving multi-tiered justice system will worsen the problem. For these reasons, the 2016 Presidential election is a de-facto election for Supreme Court Justices, and will determine the future of America.

Restore Power to the People

Restore is a computer term that means returning the operating system to an earlier version. The user has the option of picking what version of the past they want to replicate.

The American people are looking for a restore point, one the Millennials call a "reset," and are close to agreement on priorities. It would be uncomplicated if we could duplicate a past period, but the disruption has changed society forever. There is no restore point or reset. It is more logical and useful to base the restore point on values instead of a point in time. The greatest value is the Constitution.

Neither President Obama, nor any American president, is entitled to author and dictate our future without transparency and input from the people. Fraud, like the ACA and Iran agreement, are illegal regardless of who perpetrates it. The people must write the story of democracy and make sure it has a successful conclusion.

Our politicians define America in terms they understand, but that is inadequate. We are in the same quagmire, given the contention and gridlock. They suggested programs to move America ahead, bypassing the important process step of discovering what the citizens want, and developing a national mission spelling out the components of "a greater good."

The following illustration visualizes the concept of an opportunity driven society.

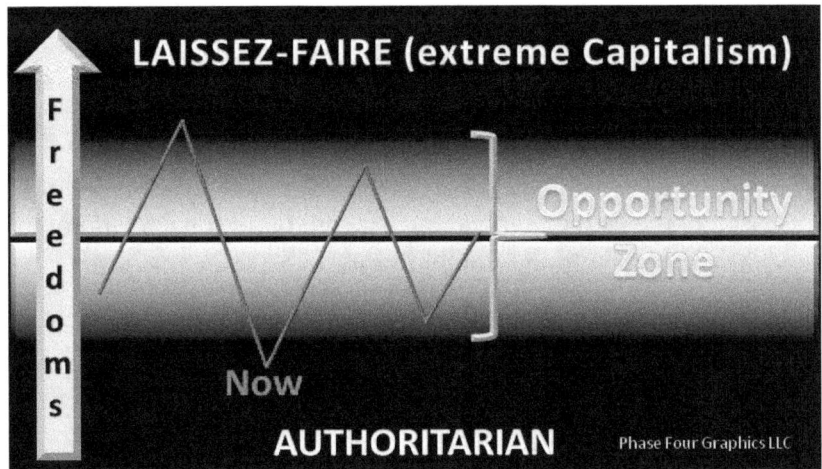

The objective is to find the right balance between competing issues. We must be free people, but believe in and practice the rule of law.

Nearly all quality systems use charts of this type, where parameters (upper and lower control limits) are established. The components of the above chart are:

Lais·sez-faire - https://www.google.com/
   1 A policy or attitude of letting things take their own course, without interfering.
   2 Abstention by governments from interfering in the workings of the free market. "laissez-faire capitalism"

Freedom - http://dictionary.reference.com
   1 The state of being <u>free</u> or at liberty rather than in confinement or under physical restraint: *He won his freedom after a retrial.*
   2 Exemption from external control, interference, regulation, etc.
   3 The power to determine action without restraint.
   4 Political or national independence.

5 Personal liberty, as opposed to bondage or slavery; *a slave who bought his freedom*.

6 Exemption from the presence of anything specified: *freedom from fear*.

7 The absence of or release from ties, obligations, etc.

Authoritarian - https://www.google.com/

1 Favoring or enforcing strict obedience to authority, especially that of the government, at the expense of personal freedom. "the transition from an authoritarian to a democratic regime" autocratic, dictatorial, despotic, tyrannical, draconian, oppressive, repressive, illiberal, undemocratic;

2 An authoritarian person. Autocrat, despot, dictator, tyrant

Interpretation

The second industrial revolution was a period of extreme laissez-faire, with all the associated negatives.

- Polluted air and water
- Entire areas poisoned with dioxin, PCBs, DDT, and asbestos.
- Labor, including child labor, poorly treated.
- Workplace safety largely ignored.

It was also a period where powerful forces of entrepreneurism built an industrial system that continues to sustain America. The factory system created the American middle class.

The opposite of unconstrained capitalism is authoritarianism, where the government manages every means of production and distribution, and controls the actions of the people. Over control and over regulation are both traits of an authoritarian state.

At one extreme, the top of the chart, there are few laws and regulations regarding capital. Everyone has complete freedom to take any action, until someone or something stops it.

On the bottom, authoritarianism, "someone" at the local, state, or national level controls every activity.

The left (Democrat) favors more government to reengineer social systems, which translates into fewer opportunities for capital and tighter control on individual and business behavior.

 The right (Republican) favors less government, greater capital opportunities, and more personal freedoms. Unconstrained, the result is the exploitation of the environment and labor.

A cynic would state it differently. Both sides are greedy - the far left for power and control, the far right for power and money. The political extreme of both sides is essentially the same, an authoritarian government.

Throughout America's short history, the conflict between too much or too little government repeats itself with a pendulum effect, but has largely remained within the range required for a free people living in an opportunity driven system.

On the chart, the band in the middle is labeled "the opportunity zone', the sweet spot between needed regulation and the freedoms required to promote entrepreneurship and enjoy liberty. An opportunity driven society finds the right balance between capital, freedoms, social needs, and the environment.

The chart indicates the U.S. is moving out of the opportunity zone and towards an authoritarian state. Reviewing the economic data for the last six years verifies the effect. The Obama administration takes an extreme position, endangering capital and freedoms, and setting the stage for further deviation from a balanced society.

Most Americans, regardless of political labels, share values that are more centrist, well within the sweet range where businesses and the people flourish. We care about each other, education, personal safety, the rule of law and freedoms. It is convenient for politicians to divide us when possible, but we must remember elected officials work for us. We want businesses to be profitable and create jobs, but reject exploitation by a bloated Wall Street.

We need the free-market principles of capitalism to drive an economic system capable of providing all the goods and services required by a modern society, and the education, health care systems and infrastructure to support it.

The only hope for the future of the entire world population depends upon the constructive application of science and technology, and true respect for planet earth.

An Action Agenda

The current administration is on an obsessive mission, and the rest of the country has not even defined a collective direction.

Ideally, Americans will agree on a shared vision and mission. It would be useful if industry, education, science, and healthcare, performed a needs assessment, then worked with the people developing options. Given the nature of the Internet, all of this is possible, and the people can participate in the definition of an inclusive "greater good," containing a national mission. As consultants, we call the process due diligence. The results would provide guidance to the legislators, who need to step back, reassess the situation, and synchronize with the people.

The rebirth of America rests with restoring the freedoms to a free market driven, opportunity-based society where entrepreneurs can build new businesses and create jobs in environmentally responsible factories and facilities. Our abundant energy, unlocked, will fuel the most productive and ecologically friendly production system in the world. As a result, the total size of the economic pie will grow larger, providing resources to recharge science, education, and health care. Most of all, it will provide opportunities for current and future generations.

The United States is the only country on earth with all the resources to lead the way into the Fourth Industrial Revolution and the prosperity it will bring to America and the world. With Canada as a partner, it has the potential to become the greatest force for good.

With a new vision of a society based on entrepreneurship, responsibility, environmental stewardship, and freedom for all, America will once again be competitive, the land of the free, the home of brave, and there will be opportunities for all.

30. *What kind of America do we want?*

Our country is in deep trouble and the future of America is very much in doubt. This year's election is pivotal, and it will determine if our Constitution continues as the law of the land, preserving our liberties, or we sink further into dystopia.

This chapter is for future generations. Its purpose is to project the macro consequences of the national election on November 8, 2016. This decision will determine how you live, what freedoms you will enjoy, and what potential opportunities will be available. The pronoun "you" is carefully used instead of the more collective "we," reflecting generational differences and opportunities. I grew up when study, hard work, good decisions, and entrepreneurism combined to create nearly unlimited opportunities. When young people made bad decisions, they were frequently able to learn and prosper from the mistakes. The government, for the most part, enabled business and personal freedoms. In fact, the Civil Rights movement justly forced the country into complying with its own Constitution. For these reasons, the struggle for liberty is not about older generations, but the kind of America citizens will establish, and their children will inherit. It is, perhaps, a form of Karma, but the people most affected by this election are the very citizens controlling the results through their votes, or non-votes. The key demographics include young adults, minorities, and women, but everyone has a role.

Options - type of government

The election involves two major governmental concepts with opposing consequences.

1   Do American voters want the freedom to control their future, or abdicate decisions to the "experts" of an ever-larger, more socialist government? It is already a bloated bureaucracy functioning to perpetuate itself, instead of working for the good of the people. The positive aspect of big government is that other people make decisions and we live with them. The government provides for the welfare of the people with more free programs administered by the government. The price that citizens pay is lost individuality, freedoms, property rights, diminished opportunities, and higher taxes. For many minorities, these programs are attractive, but as they become more successful, they become restrictions on the very opportunities they wanted in the first place. It is a demonstrated fact that America, on the path to socialism, is rapidly dividing into a two-tier economy. The top tier has the wealth and opportunities, and the lower tier becomes ever

poorer with fewer opportunities. The middle class is disappearing, suffering from declining real wages.

2   The second choice is the free enterprise systems where citizens own the government, business, property, and the means to build wealth. The advantages are that each of us controls our own destiny by hard work, good decisions, and taking advantage of opportunities to better our circumstances and ourselves. The price paid is less governmental safety nets and fewer services, but also lower taxes, and increased opportunities.

Immigrants come to America seeking opportunities, then vote for the very people that will limit those opportunities. Why seek the land of the free, and vote to make it like the country they left? Why come to America to covert us into a Mexico or Argentina?

Vision of a future America

If America is going to be successful, people need to know what kind of country they want. Before discussing the major probabilities for the future, here is my vision for America as posted on CompetitiveAmerica.us.

America must be as great for our children and grandchildren as it is/was for prior generations. Most Americans want the same basic outcomes. They want a strong economy, good jobs, a clean environment, responsible government, a viable education system, and reasonably priced health care. All are part of the American dream. Citizens deserve freedom from prejudice and unnecessary governmental regulation, freedom of religion, and freedom to pursue opportunities. That is the path to America's resurgence.

Freedom has never meant abdicating responsibility. We are stewards of our environment, resources, freedoms, and each other. Freedom is not free. It is hard work, and the intelligent use of time, resources, and personal values. It is being there for our neighbor, our military and law enforcement, firefighters, and brothers and sisters in the trench next to us.

It will take all of us to rebuild a Competitive America, and it starts by innovating the forth-industrial age, green and resource effective, led by American businesses.

> God gave America abundant resources; we must be good stewards and not bury our talents. It is our choice.

This vision is the premise for the following discussion.

Perspective on the future of America

I am pessimistic about America's future for the following reasons.

Emotions and entrenched party loyalty approaching religious fervor determined our last four elections. With tools available, such as Critical Thinking, it is hard to believe that people rejected or ignored facts that countered party bias or preconditioned opinions.

The American public, told daily that "everything" is improving, regardless of information to the contrary, believe that propaganda is a fact.

Helicopter children, coddled and protected, are dependent on resources supplied by authority figures, which may well transition from parent to government.

People are increasingly dependent on the government. It will be difficult for some demographics to take a chance on the free-enterprise system when it may negatively affect their well-being.

Perhaps the most important factor is the normalcy bias.

Normalcy bias

The normalcy bias defines how difficult it is for people to comprehend a massive, clear, and present danger. In situations counter to personal beliefs or experiences, we deny that extreme results are possible. In reality, bad things happen to people and countries all the time. No one is immune.

As a young Operating Room Technician in the Army, one of the horrible lessons learned was how rapidly situations change. A young man's heart stopped beating (cardiac arrest) during a routine tonsillectomy. When he checked into the hospital, all assumed he would spend the day in recovery and go home, instead of dying.

A three-year old child fell from a balcony, and quietly passed away to the click of medical equipment and sobs from a dozen-hospital personal surrounding the litter. The elevator door opened to evacuate her to another hospital, but no one moved, frozen in time and disbelief. The dangerous balcony had been a clear and present danger, and on that morning, the impossible occurred.

A close friend from our medical unit, an athlete and great dancer, had a car accident and his two leg bones were forced through his foot. A civilian medical protocol would have required an amputation. Our surgical team, headed by Dr. Fisher, an excellent surgeon, spent sixteen hours repairing the injury. When our friend had departed for his trip that morning, none of us imagined such a horrible accident.

In 1942, Jan Karski, a Catholic, diplomat, and member of the Polish underground, smuggled himself into a Nazi occupied Warsaw Ghetto. He discovered a horrifying genocide in progress, where the German army was exterminating the Jews, now labeled the Holocaust. He passionately reported his findings in England and America, attempting to head off this crime against humanity. The leaders of both countries refused to listen, or did not think it would happen, and six million people died horrible and preventable deaths. (Google Jan Karski and discover an unsung hero).

In 1972, a study commissioned by the Club of Rome resulted in a book titled The Limits to Growth. It was an early computer model calculating the effects of exponential human population growth against the linear discovery and availability of resources. This report, along with other works such as Rachael Carson's, Silent Spring kicked off the environmental movement, which in turn began an avalanche of change that continues to have profound effect on our society and economy.

There were multiple, predictable, consequences and here are the top two.

1   Limiting population to zero growth later created a need for additional workers in America, and enabled the influx of immigrants.

2   The off shoring of factories to other countries led to an associated job loss.

In the 1980s, the vertically integrated factory system gave way to a horizontal (global) model. People and government welcomed the transfer of polluting manufacturing operations "out of our backyard." Everyone knew that massive production job losses would occur. They ignored this reality, and instead embraced the common, but foolish, concept that high-paying knowledge jobs would make America the service capital of the world. China, a backwards third-world country, would be the benefactors of our generosity. America gave them every trade concession they asked for, without any reciprocity.

We would be the designers, thinkers, innovators, and engineers needed to manage and control these less educated emerging economies, which brilliantly took our manufacturing. The consensus, at the time, was that America would go on being the land of opportunity. The development of the Internet, a disruptive technology, allowed this intellectual interaction to occur anywhere in the world. Manufacturing support jobs, such as computer technology, followed the operations to other countries. The consequences were significant reductions in opportunities for Americans, and striking the deepest for those persons once employed in manufacturing.

This is a prime example of the normalcy bias. The consequences were, or should have been, obvious to all. At some point, the economy will go over the cliff into the abyss.

The American people appear to suffer from the normalcy bias and are in denial of the negative consequences so clearly demonstrated by numeric facts and simple arithmetic, Ref: The Digital Disruption.

Conclusion

America has slipped below the opportunity zone, and the new government will either move us back into the zone, or completely close the parameters for an opportunity driven society.

The data indicates that America cannot afford to make a mistake this election cycle. If we choose to grow the government, the country will fall into the abyss before the next election in 2020. If we elect poor leaders, they will not have the courage required to fix the problem. If they do not understand technology, they will be unable to comprehend the solutions. If they are divisive, the people will not come together and fix the problems.

We need a highly intelligent and courageous leader who will roll up the sleeves, get to work, and put American back in the zone of opportunity. As an independent, I am less concerned about party and more about individuals and policy. If they can fix America, they have my support, if not, what value do they serve as president?

Every voter needs to develop their own vision for America's future based on a study of the facts, and understanding of the consequences. If the majority of the people want big government and less freedom, so be it. However, do it on purpose, not through default, victimization, or the effects of the normalcy bias.

This election requires that people get the facts, think through the choices, and make informed, unbiased decisions. There will be consequences, and they will affect us all.

Can we avoid the abyss? I believe we can, and that is the basis for my vision and optimism for 2016, and taking the considerable time to write this book.

An updated version of this chapter will post on to CompetitiveAmerica.us on December 1, 2016. It may be a requiem for America. I pray, however, that it is a celebration, that Americans have chosen the pathway to the bright lights of future freedom and prosperity for every citizen.

The fundamental question facing America is the choice between more government and less. The extremes of either position have unacceptable consequences, even authoritarian government.

31. *Economic and Social Solutions*

I promised the little boys to find answers to "why." The reasons are an oversized bureaucracy, lack of leadership, greed, corruption, and failure to unite the people in a positive mission.

I also promised to find solutions, and have done so on a broad scale.

An Opportunity Society

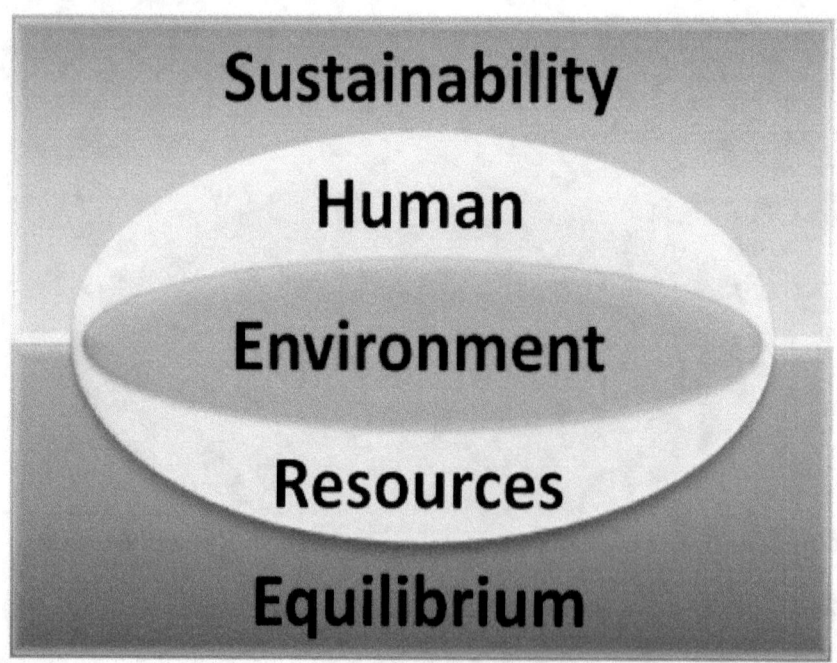

The lead icon illustrates an opportunity driven society, addressing the principles and tradeoffs of sustainability, human needs, the environment, resources, and equilibrium.

Sustainability

America must sustain itself as a nation. This requires jobs, an exceptional education system, entrepreneurs, invention, and innovation. It translates into strong industrial and service sectors, foundational for economic sustainability and increasing national power,

A strong and committed military is required to protect our lives, physical world, and our freedoms. The United States must lead the world but not police it. We must provide leadership or others will do so, specifically China, Russia, and groups like ISIS. The failure to make a decision and take positive action always means living with the default, directions determined by others, and suffer the consequences of their decisions.

We need to hold the press accountable for keeping us accurately informed. Without a free and honest press, democracy will fall. Our manipulated press now serves no purpose beyond propaganda.

Technology has been the perennial scapegoat for destroying the environment. Like money and other fungible (interchangeable) concepts, technology has application for positive or negative purposes. In this case, it will ensure the survival or destruction of the human species. There are a number of presentations on CompetitiveAmerica.us showing high-technology applications in manufacturing and food production. Manufacturing technologies, specifically miniaturization and lean programs, will reduce resource requirements. Food technology, the Green Revolution, saved millions from starving. Without advanced agriculture, many millions are destined to die. Who wants to be the person that tells them, "We want to preserve our environment for the future. I'm sorry, but that means you and your children must starve, for the greater good."

America is the most innovative country in the world and must sustain that comparative advantage. Technology, across all disciplines and fields of study, brings great opportunities for knowledge and convergence, and applied knowledge. Enterprises need to think in terms of structures and systems that promote innovation. While partially addressed by the Lean philosophy, the thought process needs to incorporate disruptive technologies, and breakthrough products, to generate situations and risks, convertible into opportunities. American industry, powered by a free society of workers and a national curiosity, will continue to be the world leader in innovation.

American manufacturers are rethinking the factory system in terms of new energy sources, automation, and the environment. The investment in advanced technologies will result in a factory system premised on energy conservation and environmental integrity.

America needs to switch its energy mix.

- There is a semi-silver bullet available but consumers have to wrap their minds around a new paradigm and force a change. America has abundant natural gas with a distribution system ninety percent in place. Given the large supplies of natural gas, switching significant transportation sectors would reduce greenhouse gases and free America from the Middle East.

- Natural gas is far more environmentally friendly than gasoline. There are restrictions, such as a shorter range for cars, but it is far greater than any electric cars. Actually, electrical generation is a major pollution contributor. With a national effort to provide a distribution system for CNG (compressed natural gas, or LNG, (liquefied natural gas) significant numbers of cars could be rapidly converted. Natural gas is also a major component and foundational for hydrogen transportation. Detroit has "off the shelf" technology. This conversion would significantly drop oil imports and hasten energy independence. The increased demand requires additional supplies.

- Americans perpetuate the billion-dollar per day outflow of dollars to the oil producing countries. Natural gas is not only a long-term solution but also a bridge-fuel available right now. For more information, enter CNG or CNG powered cars into Google.

- This switch in energy, coupled with buying from American sources takes thousands of polluting oil tankers off the earth's waterways, and reduces our risks of continually meddling in the Middle East, where they love our money but hate the freedoms we stand for. Natural gas is the bridge fuel until we can develop a new method of generating electricity.

- Create a massive research project to find a non-polluting electrical source to free the world of hydrocarbons.

- Discover a faster, effective desalinization process, needed to water crops and feed a hungry world.

- Invest in massive Infrastructure transformation with redevelopment around the Internet of Things, autonomous cars, rapid transit, and disruptive technologies. Find a way to eliminate the need for cars in the cities.

- Change education to support the needs of commerce and students. Education is about learning how to think and do things, not just "social issues."

- Restart the space program. Colonize Mars.

Human

Promote the freedoms guaranteed by the Constitution. We are a nation subject to the equal application of the Rule of Law. Elected officials take an oath to uphold and enforce the laws and are responsible and accountable to the constituents, not the people to government. When they fail at this primary task, throw them out.

Free the people to create and build on entrepreneurial opportunities without excessive intervention or regulation by government, as long as they comply with a fair set of regulations. This is an opportunity driven system with incentives and rewards worth the passion and effort required to make good things happen. This incentive fuels free enterprise, and creates businesses, services, and jobs. Slant the reward system to the producers and entrepreneurs instead of non-productive members of society. Build systems that provide food, shelter, and clothing for those in need.

Admit the numerous shortcomings in the Affordable Care Act. Restructure the health care system to provide comprehensive services at affordable prices. Start by revamping the Tort system.

Encourage entrepreneurship and innovation in education. There has been an accumulative shortage of advanced applied technology workers for ten years, yet the education system is still behind the curve. We know that bureaucracies take time to react; did that contribute to the failure to fill the education gap?

Create a student centric education system that prepares graduates for a realistic future job market. Start by returning the responsibility to the educators at the state level, who are far better prepared to educate the people than federal government bureaucrats. Use education to create equal opportunities regardless of gender, color, or religion.

Take the money spent at the federal level and return it to the states, but use it for education. Increase teachers' salaries to professional levels. Educators should not have to form a union to make an equitable salary, buy teaching materials from personal income, or ask family members to contribute extra supplies. Use the money saved by eliminating the federal bureaucracy to make quantum improvements in the schools located in troubled/poor areas. Until society can find a way to integrate low-opportunity students, equality is a buzzword.

Environment

Consumers need to educate themselves on the countries that make the products they buy. Pollution is a global issue, but as individuals, we can make a difference in our expectations and willingness to pay for a clean world. Our collective actions make a difference.

The Second industrial revolution raped the environment and companies around the world continue the practice. American industry must be ecologically responsible. It is a given, that environmental controls increase the cost of production, and global competitors save money by dumping industrial waste into the air and water. Consumers must learn to reward ecological stewardship, for example, buy from responsible American manufacturers instead of purchasing products made in polluting factories and/or using child labor.

Reduce the environmental impact of human activity. Every enterprise needs to address the environment in the governance process. The most significant issues are finding ways to cost effectively incorporate solutions into products, processes, buildings, and everyday practice.

Practice process improvement that increases yield and increase value, not just to product and process, but environmental stewardship.

Recycle everything, and reclaim what is possible.

Resources

The world is a finite sphere of eco-dependencies, filled with limited resources, multiple life forms, and endless possibilities. All systems create resource damage or waste. There are earthquakes, forest fires, and a long list of other natural disasters. Humans dig holes, spread fertilizer, cut forests, and apply chemicals, all creating waste, and environmental destruction. All human systems generate pollution of some type, such as carbon dioxide. Academics argue about the causes for global warming. The realist understands that dumping pollutants into a fixed space will eventually render it unusable, and finite resources of some types will run out.

Limited resources with increased demand create a paradox. How can humans produce and consume without destroying the environment? It appears that we have reached a lose-lose position without resolution. In spite of rhetoric, customers will continue to consume, and industry will provide goods and services. All will contribute to resource waste.

The answers are obvious and pragmatic.

- Take responsibility for resource conservation and replenishment.
- Take actions to increase productivity throughout the eco-dependencies, in the plant, office and at home.
- Recognize the importance of convergence, integrating the business enterprise to increase speed but function in sync.
- Reduce waste by buying from responsible suppliers while practicing cradle to grave recycling.

- Spend money on developing technology to create new, more sustainable materials.
- Build products designed/engineered/manufactured for recycling.
- Recycle "everything"
- Build quality products
- Repurpose where possible
- Adopt a "zero waste" attitude while knowing it is an unreachable objective

We must lead the world in scientific investigation and rapidly deploy technologies to insure clean food and water supplies, worldwide. We can contribute far more to the world with entrepreneurship and technology than by redistributing resources and energy to the point of diminishing return.

"Give a person food and teach a person how to build a fire, and they can be warm and filled until the food and fuel run out.

Teach a person how to make tools, and they will make an ax and cut the wood needed for the fire, a hoe to till the soil, and a hammer to build shelter.

Teach a person how to think, innovate, make decisions, and they can build a fire, make tools, grow food, get energy, and exploit opportunities.

Teach people how to collaborate, and they will combine knowledge, innovate, heal the sick, and break technological barriers."

America has once again become the energy center of the world. Energy cost and availability will affect products, processes, and performance. Customers and suppliers face a new set of opportunities. While there are risks in taking action, the risk of doing nothing is inconceivable. It is a simple task to look at the new energy-related technologies and find that change, and obsolescence will be pervasive as this paradigm shift gains power. The government needs to enable clean energy research, but avoid direct investments that end in disaster, such as Solyndra.

Equilibrium

Equilibrium is balance, implying responsible choices. In a civilized democracy, the people must have trust in what their government does, and confidence in a shared "for the greater good."

Develop a clear, concise direction and focused objectives, followed by a path to achieve them. The process is interactive, using the planning tools found in formal process improvement programs such as Lean.

Find a balance between the governed and the government. This is not Democrats vs. Republicans; it is we the people against the abuse of power by both parties.

Government must live within its means, with a zero national debt.

Finding a way towards balance between population, resources, and the environment will be difficult. Since 1973, the native population of America reached equilibrium with zero growth, by reducing birth rates, and nearly 50 million abortions. Immigration filled the void.

The argument about environmental equilibrium is useless unless the rest of the world joins the issue with equal zeal and commitment. It makes little sense to continue cutting opportunities for American children when we have decided, informally, to reduce our own population, redistribute our wealth, and downsize our global economic and military power. Diluted by unskilled workers, our old pay scale was undercut, a contributing factor to the reduction in take-home pay.

Opportunity

The Forth Industrial Revolution, built on environmentally friendly principles and totally obsessed with finding a natural energy source, is the only way to achieve environmental integrity without destroying humanity.

America needs leadership, a plan, and resolve to rebuild an opportunity driven economy to replace the net sum, policy-driven one we are in the process of creating. To get there, we must reject two phony premises.

First, the "new normal," a government created condition where citizens expect fewer opportunities, lower pay, and restricted personal growth. The "new normal" is the result of a policy-driven society, and the condition is not predestined or normal.

Second, people say our greatest days are behind us, and while untrue, it may become a self-fulfilling prophecy. The greatest contributing factors are the failure to learn and heed the lessons of history, the effects of societal reprogramming, and apathy.

Business, education, entrepreneurs, and concerned citizens must work together to change America to an opportunity society, and in the process regain environmental integrity.

Free enterprise

America needs a free-enterprise system that distributes wealth and opportunity by investment and capability and rewards hard work and personal initiative. Consumer demand determines winners and losers, rewarding cost-effective products manufactured in environmentally friendly facilities. Customers (we the people) establish the true value by our interaction with the marketplace. The problem is that customers, even many environmentalists, buy the lowest-cost imports without considering the source. Did production occur in sweatshops using child labor, with waste dumped into the air and water? Did we reward bad behavior? The hypocrisy is the passage of laws that drive jobs overseas, preaching a clean environment, and buying a product from offshore facilities. Perhaps environmentalism translates to "not in my backyard." The kinds of pollution creating the greatest environmental damage are global, and "out of sight, out of mind" is delusional.

There are Americans who have lost faith that God has blessed our country. Just as the world reached theoretical peak oil production, and we were about to suffer enormous increases in energy prices, a technological miracle occurred in the discovery of greater than one hundred year's supply of natural gas. This discovery, and the wealth and influence it generates, will be the foundation for our economic recovery after Obama leaves office. Free enterprise, science, and education must use technology as a bridge opportunity for the development of environmentally friendly energy sources. The world may not get another chance and independence from hydrocarbons must remain an international objective. God gave us time. Saved from redistribution and downsizing, let us not waste our opportunity.

Solutions must prevent environmental degradation

Free enterprise cannot allow greed for money and power to govern who we are as people. Manufacturing must build environmentally friendly facilities and products. The populace must learn if they want a clean environment to buy from green factories, even if paying more.

To achieve these changes, American must have the same courage as our founders, and change the direction our country is heading. We have the Constitution and a Bill of Rights but we need new leadership willing to take the bold steps into a future filled with both high risk and

When America is strong and independent and its entrepreneurial spirit free to develop we will once again pursue the rewards of the great American experiment.

We can and must preserve those wilderness areas where our spirits can reach up and touch God's fingertips, and leave a legacy of clean air and water to the future generations of the world.

Thank you, God.

General Sherman - Sequoia National Park, CA
Photograph - Wayne L Staley

America's better days can be ahead.
While God gave us the resources, it is
up to us to use them wisely and
morally.

We are responsible for making
intelligent decisions and we are
accountable for the consequences.

Bibliography

Albrecht, Karl,.*Successful Management by Objectives*

Alesina, Alberto, Angeletos, George-Marios,.*Fairness and Redistribution: US versus Europe*

Ali, Ayaan Hirsi,. *Infidel*

Alinski, Saul D.,.*Rules for Radicals: A Practical Primer for Realistic Radicals*

Allsopp, Bruce,.*The Garden Earth - The Case for Ecological Morality*

Andrews, Kenneth R.,.*The Concept of Corporate Strategy*

Anger, Gene,.*Rewire Your Brain for Success*

Aronoff , Roger,.*Media Hits and Misses Covering Benghazi Press Conference*

Aronoff, Roger,.*VA Crises Getting Lost in Scandal Overload*

Arthur, Brain, . *Increasing Returns and the New World of Business*

Article II Section 2 of the *U.S. Constitution*

Asimov, Isaac,.*I, Robot*

Atschuller, Genrich,.*40 Principles-TRIZ Keys to Technical Innovation*

Attkisson, Sharyl,.*Stonewalled: My Fight for Truth Against the Forces of Obstruction, Intimidation, and Harassment in Obama's Washington*

Atwood,Margaret,. *The Handmaid's Tale*

Batley, Melanie,.*Email Shows Adviser Urged Rice to Blame Video for Benghazi Attack*

BCG Boston Consulting Group,.*Made in America, Again: Why Manufacturing will return to the U.S.*

Beamon, Todd,.*Inhofe: Benghazi 'Worst of All Cover-ups'*

Blanchard, Kenneth, Miller, Mark,.*Great Leaders Grow: Becoming A Leader for Life*

Blanchard, Kenneth, PhD, Johnson, Spencer MD,. *One Minute Manager*

Blelloch, Guy,.*Parallel Thinking*

Bono, Edward,.*DATT (Direction Attention Thinking Tools)*

Bono, Edward,.*Effective Thinking*

Bowie, Mary Jo., Schaffer Regina., *Understanding ICD-10 and ICD-10-PC*

Bradbury, Ray,.*Fahrenheit 451*

Burton, Fred, Katz Samuel M.,.*Under Fire: The Untold Story of the Attack in Benghazi*

Burwell, Mark,.*The Evolutionary Entrepreneur-Beyond the Passion*

Butler, Octavia E.,. *Parable of the Sower*

Byman, Daniel,.*Terrorism in North Africa: Before and After Benghazi*

Carson, Rachel,.*Silent Spring*

Champy, Jim,.*Radically Rethinking Business Delivery*

Charan, Ram,.*What the CEO Wants You to Know*

Chicago Booth/Kellogg School Financial Trust Index

chron.com/news/nation-world/nation/article/Americans

Cleary, Thomas,.*The Japanese Art of War*

Cockburn, Patrick,.*The Jihadis Return: ISIS and the New Sunni Uprising*

Cooney, Scott,.*What Does Entrepreneurship Really Come Down To? An Interview With Stephen M.R. Covey*

Cooper, Robin,Slagmulder, Regine,.*Supply Chain Development for the Lean Enterprise*

Costhelper.com

Cotter, John P.,.*Leading Change*

Cotter, John P.,.*The New Rules*

Covey, Stephen R.*The 7 Habits of Highly Effective People*

Covey, Steven R.,.*Principle Centered Leadership*

Crosby, Philip B.,.*Quality is Free*

Crouch, Margot,.*Breaking Business Research: "Accountable Care" Unlikely*

csoonline.com/article/2130877/data-protection/the-15-worst-data-security-breaches-of-the-21st-century.html

Dawson, Roger,.*The 13 Secrets of Power Performance*

de Bono, Edward,.*Lateral Thinking for Management*

Delbecq, Andre L, Van de Ven, A.H. Gustafson, David H..,*Group Techniques for Program Planning*

Dick, Phillip K.,.*Do Androids Dream of Electric Sheep?*

Doob, Leonard W.,.*Goebbels' Principles of Propaganda*

Dow Chemical,. *Quality Performance*

Drucker, Peter F.,.*Technology, Management and Society*

Drucker, Peter,.*The Frontiers of Management*

ECGpedia,.*ST Morphology*

Esri.com,.*Using Location Intelligence to Maximize the Value of BI* esri.com/software/arcgis -ArcGIS Platform - *Innovation through GeographyPew Forum on Religion & Public Life / U.S. Religious Landscape Survey*

Etzioni, Amitai,.*Complex Organizations*

fcit.coedu.usf.edu/holocaust/timeline/nazirise.htm

feedingamerica.org/.

Gallo, Carmine,.*Innovate the Steve Jobs Way*

Gates, Bill,.*Business at the Speed of Thought*

Gates, Robert M,.*Duty: Memoirs of a Secretary of War*

Gerald, Nader, PhD,Shozo, Hibini, PhD, John, Farrell,.*Breakthrough Thinking: The Seven Principles of Creative Problem Solving*

Gergersen, Jeff Dyer Hal, Christensen, Clayton M.,. *Five Discovery Skills that Distinguish Great Innovators*

Gingrich, Newt,Maple, Terry L,.*A Contract with the Earth*

Goldratt, Eliyahu M.,. *Theory of Constraints*

Goldratt, Eliyahu M.,.*It's Not Luck*

Goldratt, Eliyahu M.,Cox, Jeff,.*The Goal*

Gordon, Edward E.*Future Jobs- Solving the Employment and Skill Crisis*

Gordon, Edward E.*The 2010 Meltdown*

Greenberg, Paul,.*CRM At The Speed of Light*

Greenfield, Daniel,.*Benghazi's Tough Questions*

Griffin, Douglas, Stacey, Ralph,. *Complexity and the Experience of Leading Organizations*

Grossman, Lee,*The Change Agent*

Gunn, Thomas G.,.*Computer Applications in Manufacturing*

Hammer, Michael,.*Beyond Reengineering*

Hammer, Michael,.*The Reengineering Revolution*

Hartung, Adam,.*Why the Pursuit of Innovation Usually Fails*

Harvard University, Christensen, Clayton M.,.*A Disruptive Solution for Business Advanced Leadership Inst*

Harvard University's Institute of Politics

Hawken Paul,Lovins, Amory,Lovins, L Hunter,. *Natural Capitalism - Creating The Next Industrial Revolution*

Hayden, Catherine,.*The Handbook of Strategic Expertise*

Hazy, J.K.,*Forms of Social organization and Leadership – Insights into individuals and complex organizations*

historylearningsite.co.uk/*propaganda_in_nazi_germany*

Hitler, Adolf,.*Mein Kampf*

Holocaust Timeline: *The Rise of the Nazi Party*

Hout, Carrie.,*An Integrated Planning Model in Business: From Vision to Reality*

Hubbert, M. King,.*Two Intellectual Systems: Matter-energy and the Monetary Culture*

hubbertpeak.com/hubbert/1956/1956.pdf

huffingtonpost.com/2012/08/23/survey-many-teachers-repo_n_1822777.html

Huxley, Aldous,. *Brave New World*

ideationtriz.com,.*Introduction to Basic I-TRIZ*

Inglehart, Ronald,Welzel, Christian,.*The Inglehart-Weizel Cultural Map of the World*

Institute of Medicine,. *To Err is Human: Building a Safer Health System*

Intoccia, Gregory Francis,.*American Bombing of Libya: An International Legal Analysis*

James P. Womack, Jones, Daniel T.,.*Lean Thinking*

Japan Management Association,.*Kanban – Just In Time at Toyota*

jonathanturley.files.wordpress.com

Judicial Watch,. *Judicial Watch Sues DOJ for Operation Choke Point Records*

Kafka, Franz,.*The Trial*

Kellar, Dan,. *A Redistribution of Wealth: A moral issue*

Kelley,Tom, Littman, Jonathan,. *The Art of Innovation*

Kirkpatrick, Donald L.,.*How to Manage Change Effectively*

Lawson, Nigel,.*The Economics and Politics of Climate Change an Appeal to Reason*

Leahy, Michael Patrick,.*Obama's 'Operation Choke Point' Seeks to Destroy Sectors of Private Lending Industry*

Lopez, Clare,.*Material Support to Terrorism: The Case of Libya*

Malthus, Thomas Robert,.*An Essay on the Principle of Population*

Martosko, David,.*Benghazi attack could have been prevented if US hadn't 'switched sides in the War on Terror' and allowed $500 MILLION of weapons to reach al-Qaeda militants*

Maslow, Abraham,.*A Theory of Human Motivation*

mazur.net/triz/,.*The Theory of Inventive Problem Solving*

McKinsey Global Institute,. *Big Data: The Next Frontier for Innovation, Competition, and Productivity*

Meadows, Donella H., Meadows Dennis L., Randers, Jorgen and BehrensIII, William W,. *The Limits to growth; a Report for the Club of Rome's Project on the Predicament of Mankind*

Meyers, Arlen,.*Skills of Successful Entrepreneurs*

Mintzberg, Henry,.*The Rise and Fall of Strategic Planning*

Moore, Geoffrey A.,.*Crossing the Chasm*

Morell, Michael,.*Report: Ex-CIA Deputy Director May Have Altered Benghazi Talking Points*

Motorola,.*Six Sigma*

Muirhead, Brian K, Simon, William L.,.*High Velocity Leadership*

nejm.org/doi/full/10.1056/NEJMp1403294

newsbusters.org/blogs/melissa-mullins/2014/10/31/*usa-todays-susan-page-obama-team-most-dangerous-press-us-history#sthash.aViAStJK.dpuf*

ninds.nih.gov,.*Know Your Brain*

Numerof, Rita Ph.D.,.*Why Accountable Care Organizations Won't Deliver Better Business – And market Innovation Will*

nytimes.com/2013/11/25/*booming/love-canal-and-its-mixed-*

legacy.html

Obama, Barack,.*The Audacity of Hope: Thoughts on Reclaiming the American Dream*

Ohmae, Kenichi,.*The Mind of the Strategist*

Omachonu, Vincent K, Einspruch, Norman G.,.*Innovation in Business Delivery Systems: A Conceptual Framework*

online.wsj.com/articles/*sony-pictures-hack-reveals-more-data-than-previously-believed-1417734425*

Orlovsky, Christina,.*Five Key Trends in Business Technology*

Orwell, George,.*Nineteen Eighty-Four*

Ostry, Jonathan D., Berg, Andrew, Tsangarides, Charalambos G.,.*Redistribution, Inequality, and Growth*

Panetta, Leon,.*Worthy Fights: A Memoir of Leadership in War and Peace*

pbs.org/newshour/bb/science-jan-june11-databreach_04-27/

pegasuscom.com,.*From Fragmentation to Integration: Building Learning Communities*

Peters, Tom,.*Liberation Management*

Pittman, Paul H. PhD, Atwater, J. Brian.PhD,.*Managing Dynamic Complexity: The Foundation of TPS*

politico.com/story/2014/01/*contraceptive-mandate-obamacare-little-sisters-for-the-poor-supreme-court-102587.*html

Posner, Rov,.*The Power of Personal Values*

Presidential Oath of Office, Military Officers, Enlisted Personnel

Rand, Ayn,. *Atlas Shrugged*

reason.com/blog/2014/07/24/watch-obamacare-architect-jonathan-gruber

redalertpolitics.com/2014/11/10/*obamacare-architect-jonathan-gruber-law-passed-thanks-lack-transparency*

Reporters Without Borders,. *U.S. Drops to 47th on Press Freedom Index; Annual Press Freedom Index*

Rezak, Catherine J, Kathleen Hurson, Kathleen., *New Leadership Thinking in Play – Simulation Develops Leadership*

Richards Chet,., *Surprise and Anticipation: The Principles of War as Applied to Business*

Robinson, Dana Gaines, Robinson, James C,.. *Performance*

Consulting : Moving Beyond Training

Rothschild, Michael,.*Bionomics: Economy as Ecosystem*

Schonberger, Richard J.,.World Class Manufacturing: *The Lessons of Simplicity Applied*

Senge, Peter The Fifth Discipline: *The Art and Practice of the Learning Organization*

Senge, Peter,.*The Tragedy of Our Time*

Shapiro, Ben,.Barack Obama, *Judge of Life or Death*

Shiva, Vandana,.*Soil Not Oil - Environmental Justice in a Time of Climate Crisis*

Silverthorne, Sean,. *Lessons Not Learned About Innovation*

Slywotzky, Adrian J,.*Value Migration*

Smalley, Art,.*A3 Thinking and Standardized Work*

SolutionHiebeler, Robert, Kelly, Thomas B, Ketterman, Charles,. *Best Practices : Building Your Business With Customer Focused*

Staley, John Eric,.*Goals in Effective Communications and Public Speaking*

Szymankiewicz, Jan, McDonald James,Turner, Keith,. *Solving Business Problems by Simulation*

Terninko, John,Zusman, Alla,Zlotin, Boris,.*Systematic Innovation: An Introduction to Triz*

The Bill of Rights

The Declaration of Independence

The Globalist,. *The New Religion of Eco-Fundamentalism?*

Toffler, Alvin and Heidi,.*War and Anti-War - Survival at the Dawn of the 21st Century*

Toussaint, John MD., Gerard, Roger A. PhD., Adams, Emily,. *On the Mend - Revolutionizing Health Car*

townhall.com/columnists/johnhawkins/

Tregoe Benjamin B., Zimmerman, John W.,*Top Management Strategy What it is and How to Make It Work*

Uravic, Ed,.*Lying Cheating Scum*

variety.com/2014/film/news/hackers-threaten-sony-employees-in-new-email-your-family-will-be-in-danger-1201372230/

variety.com/2014/film/news/*sony-hack-unparalleled-cyber-security-firm-1201372889/Sony Hack*

Waldrop, M. Mitchell,.*Complexity – The Emerging Science at the Edge of Order and Chaos*

Walker, William T. Crandell , Richard E., PhD., *Blurring Manufacturing and Service Boundaries*

Wheatley, Margaret J., *Leadership and the New Science: Learning about Organization from an Orderly Universe*

Weiss, Rusty,.*Private Companies Mimic Government's 'Choke Point' Program*

Wellins, Richard S, Byham, William C, Dixon, George R.,. *Inside Teams – How 20 World-Class Organizations are Winning Through Teamwork*

Whiteley, Richard, Hessan, Diane,.*Customer Centered Growth-Five Strategies for Building Competitive Advantage*

Wight, Oliver W,.*MRPII Unlocking America's Productivity Potential*

Wilson, Edward O., *Consilience: The Unity of Knowledge*

wkrn.com/story/21858334/ *study-finds-teachers...pocket-on-supplies*

Womak, James,Jones, Daniel, Roo, Daniel,. *The Machine That Changed the World*

Yousafzai, Malala, Lamb, Christina,.*I Am Malala: The Girl Who Stood Up for Education and Was Shot by the Taliban*

Zangwill, Willard L.,.*Lightning Strategies for Innovation*

Zebra Technologies,.*The Factory of the Future -A practical guide to harnessing new value in manufacturing*

Index

251

257

About the Author

Wayne Staley established Affinity Systems LLC, a system consulting company, in 1997.

Educated in computer technology,   business, and manufacturing systems, Wayne managed Corporate Information Technology, Materials, and Logistics, for multi-plant, vertically integrated metal processing and forest products manufacturing corporations. His experience includes Manager of Shop Operations for a complex fabrication facility.

Certified in TQM, NAFTA, and Project Management, Wayne audited Mexican operations, worked on integrated supply chain programs with Chinese suppliers, and collaboration programs with Dow Chemical, developing processes and new products. He performed numerous studies on energy, products, and doing business in Mexico. He served for eleven years on the City/County information processing commission.

He has managed numerous projects, including business strategy, Enterprise Resource Planning (ERP), and Lean (VMP) in manufacturing, government, distribution, and convention management.

He created Phase Four Graphics LLC, phasefourgraphics.com, and CompetitiveAmerica.us, advocating for American industry. Phase Four Graphics LLC developed training materials for ERP, Supply-Chain Management, Strategy, and Process Improvement. Wayne is a member of the Society Manufacturing Engineering, and a past member of APICS and AITP. He has presented at meetings, conferences, and seminars, for all three. He has authored seven books.

Our Publications

Decision Making in a Disruptive Reordering

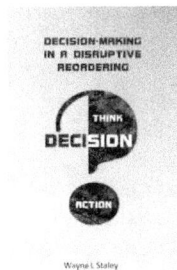

Technology has changed our world forever, but the disruption has only begun.

Automation is changing the workplace, and human jobs are being replaced by machines. These changes also disrupt the education system.

Entrepreneurship represents the path to success for many people. This requires recognizing and taking advantage of opportunities. The common denominator for success in a disruptive world is developing good decision-making skills.

"They" will do Anything-Identity Theft and Internet Fraud

- Who are THEY?
- What do THEY want?
- How do THEY get it?
- How do THEY use it?
- What can we do to prevent it?

Identity theft and internet fraud are two of the most significant problems faced by individuals and society. With the explosion of technology into the "internet of things", everyone is in danger. There is no choice. As individuals we must take actions to protect ourselves, our digital identities, and our digital clones.

ERP Lessons Learned-Structured Process

ERP projects are tough work but very important for the future of your company. Competitive pressures will only intensify, and companies will compete at ever-faster speeds.

Those serving as project team members, directly or on functional teams, hold the operational effectiveness of your employer in your hands. As you take actions to get the job done, the outcome will affect many lives.

ERP Structured Process, forged in the heat of project management, is not an intellectual exercise, but a systematic guide to executing a successful project. It starts with understanding operations, and ends with successful operational systems.

ERP Information at the Speed of Reality

Every type of business must execute effectively and move from a physical and information reality of weeks and days to minutes and seconds. The smart enterprise builds intelligence gathering in near real time, taking full advantage of faster operations.

ERP projects are complex, involving strategies, internal assessments, evaluation of multiple alternatives, and making critical business decisions. They require assigning high performers to project teams, taking them away from important daily activities. ERP systems are so expensive that failure is not an option. Evidence based decisions and a structured process lead to successful results.

Pathway to Adaptability

The marketplace demands correct products, appropriately priced and available now. Speed is King! Enterprises must become very smart, building real-time intelligence into every activity. Without accurate information foundations, and process improvement, adaptability is not achievable and significant opportunities will be lost.

"This book has invaluable information on LEAN Six Sigma Methodology that is used in my company, and has been used as a reference point in many of our LEAN Focus Groups across the country. I highly recommend Wayne Staley's book." Amazon review by Black Belt.

Freedom and Opportunity-Stop Redistributing and Downsizing America

The current greatest barriers to growth are the policies of the Federal government, quickly followed by the forgotten or unlearned lessons of history. We are all part of the problem, and building a viable America demands positive actions. If we fail to rekindle the America dream, it is our fault - yours and mine and every citizen of America.

Coupled with Canada by geography, demographics, and economy, North America can become the opportunity capital of the world. It will take positive leadership, courage, and a government that enables entrepreneurs and business instead of imposing penalties, redistributing wealth and power, and downsizing America.

The primary mission of health care professionals, executive leadership, and associates is delivering quality health care to patients.

Productivity Prescriptions for Health Care provides a structured program methodology for defining and implementing contemporary process improvement programs specifically designed for the special requirements of health care organizations.

Productivity improvement programs are required for future Health care sustainability, with quality and efficiency the twins for success.

261